THE "FRENCH WRITERS OF CANADA" SERIES

The purpose of this series is to bring to English readers, for the first time, in a uniform and inexpensive format, a selection of outstanding and representative works of fiction by French authors in Canada. Individual titles in the series will range from the most modern work to the classic. Our editors have examined the entire repertory of French fiction in this country to ensure that each book that is selected will reflect important literary and social trends, in addition to having evident aesthetic value.

(continued inside back cover)

The Complete Poems of Emile Nelligan

translated and
with an introduction by
Fred Cogswell

Copyright © 1983 by Harvest House Ltd.

First Harvest House Edition. *The Complete Poems of Emile Nelligan* was first published in the French language by La Corporation Des Éditions Fides of Montreal, under the title, *Poésies Complètes*.

Printed in Canada. Deposited in the Bibliothèque Nationale of Quebec, 2nd quarter, 1983.

Typography and cover: Naoto Kondo.

Series design: Robert Reid.

Canadian Cataloguing in Publication Data
Nelligan, Emile, 1879–1941
    The complete poems of Emile Nelligan

(The French writers of Canada series)
ISBN 0–88772–218–0

I. Cogswell, Fred, 1917–   II. Title.   III. Series.

PS8477.E4A17   1982   C841'.4   C83–090000–4
PQ3919.N44A17   1982

To David

Contents

xii

Acknowledgments

Harvest House wishes to acknowledge the co-operation of Gilles Corbeille, president of La Fondation Emile Nelligan, who authorized this English language version of Emile Nelligan's *Poésies Complètés* on behalf of the foundation.

The editor and publishers also gratefully acknowledge a translation grant from the Canada Council.

Emile Nelligan

Between the years 1896 and 1899, an unhappy bewildered boy wrote poems in Montreal before succumbing to madness. When I first read these poems in their entirety, I came to the conclusion that their author was the finest poet writing in Canada in the nineteenth century and, in terms of sensibility and use of images as a correlative for his private feelings, the first modern Canadian poet. I have put together many hours of concentration to translate his poems. I hoped that by so doing I should make them available to an English speaking audience and thereby persuade many who might not otherwise do so to look at them in the original where they shine in their true glory.

Emile Nelligan was born on 24 December, 1879, in Montreal. His father was David Nelligan who, at the age of twelve, had come with his father to Canada from Ireland. His mother, Emilie-Amanda, was the daughter of Joseph-Magloire Hudon, advocate and first mayor of Rimouski. Emile was the couple's first child and their only son. A daughter, Gertrude, was born four years later.

David Nelligan was a practical, sensible, busy man who rose to become an Inspector of Post Offices in the Province of Quebec. Emilie-Amanda was a sensitive woman who loved music, poetry, and her children; she was, moreover, a devout

Roman Catholic. Since throughout childhood and adolescence, Nelligan saw little of his father who, by the nature of his profession, was almost constantly absent from home, the most constant factor in his life was the ambience provided by a loving mother and a young adoring sister. There was during these years no ground at all for alienation between the future poet and his environment.

In the fall of 1886, Nelligan entered l'Ecole Olier on Park Avenue. In 1891, he became a day pupil at Mont St. Louis. In 1893, he was enrolled in Latin elements at the Petit Séminaire de Montréal. In 1896, he was enrolled in the Collège Sainte-Marie as a day student. He remained there until January, 1897, when he failed his examinations for the first semester. This concluded his schooling.

The history of Nelligan's schooling as recorded in marks and attendance records is a spotty one. On a few occasions, he was absent from classes for long periods; these usually coincided with the close of the Christmas vacation or the beginning of the Summer vacation, which his family annually spent in the country. That he could be an excellent student was demonstrated by his prize-winning years, 1895 at the Petit Séminaire, and 1896 at the Collège Sainte-Marie. That, in the final analysis, his heart was not in academic studies but very much elsewhere was proven by his final grades in 1897 when he received 379 points out of a possible 900.

This pattern which emerges from Nelligan's school days is one in which a child from a good home with habitual docility achieves relative excellence during his early school days only to culminate in failure when, for the first time in his life, an interest outside his immediate family consumes him entirely. The influence in this case was a highly impractical one, the reading and writing of poetry.

When a seventeen-year-old fails his academic examinations, and thereby thwarts the ambitions (for his only son's future) of a practical ambitious civil servant, the result is to bring a jarring end to the innocent paradise of childhood and to bring into being a prolonged crisis out of which can only come sharp feelings of alienation, self-contempt, hopelessness, and despair.

On at least two occasions, David Nelligan tried to ensure a workaday future for his poet son. In the Summer of 1898, he procured him a job on a boat sailing to Liverpool and back. When, on his return two months later, Emile decided the sea was not his metier, David found him a post as clerk in an office. Emile quit this within a week. His father then left him to his own devices, hoping no doubt that, through acquaintance with the literary world, his son would become disillusioned, return to his senses, and buckle down to some sort of steady remunerative employment.

The result, within the psyche of Emile Nelligan, was a titanic inner struggle — a struggle that was to produce the first modern poetry to be written in Canada and at the same time to destroy its creator.

Whether written in French or in English, nineteenth century poetry in Canada was intrinsically different from that written today in both languages. Then, the poet was thought of primarily as the public voice or mouthpiece of the beliefs and aspirations of a unified society. Even when a poet used an incident from his private life or expressed a personal feeling, any alienation was submerged in an overall acceptance of the general mores and sensibility. There were, however, poets elsewhere who stood for something different — something which in time came to stand for a forerunnership of modernity. Most of them were poets who wrote in French, the heirs or "cousins" of that unhappy isolated American genius, Edgar Allan Poe: Baudelaire, Rimbaud, Verlaine, Rodenbach, Rollinat. These were available and read by most of Nelligan's educated contemporaries, whether they were French or English. They were, I would suggest, read by these others in a different sense from that in which Nelligan read them. "A fool does not see the same tree that a wise man does," wrote William Blake, and the works of powerful alienated geniuses, although they appeal to latent frustrations within the psyches of all men, do not ordinarily disturb the appearance of reality within the psyches of most, who have found, consciously or unconsciously, a *modus vivendi* that seems to work well in their own lives. If, however, they are read by some one as confused, tormented, and alienated as themselves, they can be to that poor soul both a message from kindred spirits and beacons to further creative endeavour. Such a poor soul Emile Nelligan must have been at the time when, during his last year at school, he made their acquaintance, and the events of the subsequent three years must have deepened and sharpened their influence.

Emile Nelligan had to face, at one and the same time, the self-disgust and self-contempt over the loss of innocence that comes with adolescence —

the knowledge that in his thoughts, desires, and in some of his actions he was very far indeed from being what the mother he had so loved had taught him that he ought to be. He had, moreover, to face the growing knowledge that he had disappointed his father, that he was a parasite on his family, that for all practical purposes he was useless, a failure. He was further frustrated by his shyness and could only love in silence and in verse the neighbour's daughter who compelled his adolescent adoration. Prompted by a friend, Arthur de Buissières, he was introduced in 1897 to the recently founded l'Ecole Littéraire de Montreal but could find so little of interest in it that he was suspended for non-attendance and had formally to be re-admitted to membership. Even in his attempts to find publication for his poems, he suffered disappointment. Most of his work remained unpublished during his lifetime, and, had it not been for his friendship with Père Eugène Seers (Louis Dantin), it is conceivable not only that many of the poems published during his lifetime but also the bulk of his work might not have found publication at all.

In a quite natural deference on the part of a youthful poet to the power of literary tradition, Nelligan did strive manfully to become a public poet. He seldom broke with established forms. His most frequently used vehicle of expression is the sonnet, and the most common metrical form that his lines take is the alexandrine. Moreover, in two of his most obsessive themes, the celebration of childhood and the celebration of religious piety, he is, in attitude and sensibility, orthodox and contemporary. [The young adolescent imbibed the conventional attitudes of his time, including the prejudice contained in his poems, "The Deicides," "Supper's King," and "The Antique Dealer."] Both celebrations, however, are valedictories. The paradise of childhood and its innocence are lost; he is no longer a child, hence no longer innocent. So, too, is it with religious miracles and piety; the age of miracles is in the past, and he is incapable of the religious devotion of his Carmelites or even of his mother. What then is left of a positive and public nature with which to build? Marriage, work, and a family of his own seem to be beyond even his imagination. All that remains are nightmares, states of anxiety, fear and disgust often expressed in bizarre landscapes private to himself, and praise for the poets and musicians of the world who unlock the doors of feeling and immerse one so deeply in the momentary sensation that the unanswerable problems of the human condition are forgotten.

It is in these bizarre nightmare landscapes expressed with such felicity of language and rhythm as to seem inevitable that Nelligan's true greatness as a poet lies. Much has been written about his often anthologized "Ship of Gold" with its blend of exotic surrealism and prophetic foreboding, and the praise is justified. To me, however, Nelligan's masterpiece is "Tawny Landscape" where hunger, savagery, cold, and snow combine to paint an apocalypse of Northern alienation beautiful in its surreal madness.

Madness came. I shall quote below from P. F. Widdows introduction to *Selected Poems* (1960):

During the last year of his poetic career, 1899, Nelligan experienced a sense of mounting tension between himself as an artist and the uncomprehending society in which he lived. He had already had premonitions of disaster, had even said to Louis Dantin, "Je mourrai fou — comme Baudelaire." The occasion which led to his eventual collapse was in itself rather trivial. A visiting French journalist, E. de Marchy, made some adverse criticism of his poem "Le Perroquet" at a meeting of l'Ecole Littéraire. Nelligan took this criticism very hard; took it, it seems, as an epitome of the brute world's opposition to the poet. Some two months later, on May 26, at a public meeting of l'Ecole Littéraire Nelligan read "La Romance du Vin," his answer to de Marchy, his manifesto. Louis Dantin was present and has described the scene: "When, with eyes blazing and with gestures exaggerated by his inner excitement, he declaimed his "Romance du Vin," in passionate tones, a genuine thrill of emotion gripped the hall, and the applause took on the frenzy of an ovation." Afterwards his colleagues carried him home on their shoulders.

It was his last appearance at l'Ecole Littéraire. His reason began to fail. He wandered about reciting scraps of poetry: he passed sleepless nights, or nights haunted by sinister dreams which he wrote down as poems the next day. ("Vision" is from this period.) Finally, on August 9 his parents took him to La Retraite Saint Benoit, suffering from a nervous disorder which was later described, on his transfer in 1925 to l'Hôpital Saint-Jean-de-Dieu, as dementia praecox. He lived from 1899 until his death in 1941 in a state of remote indifference. Visits of friendship and homage were paid to him, but he could only concentrate for short periods. Correctly had Louis Dantin opened his essay on Nelligan in 1902 with the words "Emile Nelligan est mort." The prophecy of "Le Vaisseau d'Or" had been true.

Between 1899 and 1903, Nelligan's friend, Louis Dantin, laboured under difficult circumstances to bring out *Emile Nelligan et son oeuvre,* which appeared in 1904. The work was favourably received both in Canada and in France.

From time to time, newly discovered poems and fragments of Nelligan's work were published. A second edition of *Emile Nelligan et son oeuvre* appeared in 1925, a third edition in 1932, and *Poésies,* a fourth edition was published in 1945. The standard edition is *Poésies Complètes,* text established and annotated by Luc Lacourcière, published by Fides, Montreal and Paris, 1945.

In 1960, the Ryerson Press of Toronto published *Selected Poems,* translated into English by P. F. Widdows. This book contains a generally good translation of thirty-two poems and an excellent introduction.

Mine is the first complete translation of the standard canon of Nelligan's poetry with which I consider to be English equivalent verse.

FRED COGSWELL
University of New Brunswick
Fredericton, N.B.

The Poet's Soul

The Mind's Moonlight

In distant lights my coloured thoughts unfold
Out of some crypt of undetermined deep.
Sometimes in fine luxuriance they sweep
Up from a gulf where sunbeams drop their gold.

Through smells and quiet nights their lives are told
In echoing gardens where the fountains weep;
In distant lights my coloured thoughts unfold
Out of some crypt of undetermined deep.

They run forever on white ways that hold
Toward that angelic land where fervours leap;
Far from the squalor of this material heap
They dream a flight to heavenly Athens old.

My thoughts are coloured moons of distant gold.

My Soul

My soul is as artless as a flake of snow
      In February . . .
Ah! back to childhood's threshold let us go,
      Please come with me . . .

Join fingers, weep and pray and dream, my dear,
    As in the old days
When in my room at eve your words rose clear
    To Mary's coloured face.

Ah! how unlucky is an artless soul
In this false, dull, and crooked world below,
To have a soul that, like the Winter snow,
By vile delights has never been made foul!

To have a soul like the white linen frill
That to a convent novice nun belongs,
Or like a lute laden with soft wind-songs
That breathe and sigh at evening on the hill!

To have a soul, a gentle mystic, tender thing,
Bearing yet all ills that await us here,
Our living in sorrow, our dying in fear,
Hoping, believing . . . and always our waiting!

Ship of Gold

Hewn out of solid gold, a tall ship sailed:
Its masts reached up to heaven, on unknown seas;
Venus, naked, her hair cast to the breeze,
In scorching sun, stood at the prow unveiled.

But then one night on Ocean's cheating wave
While Sirens sang, it struck a reef head on,
And dreadful shipwreck beat its hull right down
To the depths of the gulf, that rigid grave.

A gold ship, whose translucence in each part
Disclosed the treasures that those impious tars,
Disgust and Hate and Madness, fought to keep.

How much remains after the storm's brief wars?
And what of that deserted craft, my heart?
In Dream-Abyss, alas, it foundered deep!

2

The Garden of Childhood

Yesterday's Keyboard

I call up a few days of old,
Memory's keyboard-ring,
And my own child's Eden of gold

Rises with its very own Spring,
Smiling out of hope's pure mould,
And the music of dreams that sing . . .

Now you are sadly slain,
My muse of bright endeavour,
It is for you I ache with pain;

And it is for you that ever
So many wailing songs complain
On the harsh lute of your lover.

Before My Cradle

In a big old room with its linen screens,
Where the silk was sullied and the brocade torn,
Amid sorrow's trappings there I was born,
And its pure pearled ghost is sealed in my veins.

A choking obsession sobbed strong in my head,
So bitter in me these memories were,

When, recalling my mother's loving care,
Yesterday, I bent over my childhood bed.

When this bad world's threshold I scarcely crossed,
Cradle, what dire cloths did you weave for me?
My life is a shield on walls of misery;
Where I go now my wretched feet are lost.

Your swaddling clothes do not compose my
      shroud,
Nor from your white wood frail is shaped my bier
When, all a-tremble, bent above me here,
My mother smiles amid an angel crowd.

Nostalgia for Toys

My heart still keeps a sadness graven there,
Affection for that winsome child for whom
Death blew upon his hunting horn of doom
Because she was so lovely, sweet, and fair.

Like a northern prince inside his Kremlin's lair,
Since then I feel walled-in against the world,
And, choked with grief around my heart-strings
      curled,
Love no longer swells as in my seventh year.

Whereto has fled that day of childhood folderols,
When Lucille and I were jumping jacks for fun
In crumpled clothes together on the run?

The little girl has climbed beyond the moon,
And I have lost my pride in dressing dolls . . .
Ah! to pass the gate of twenty years so soon!

Before the Fire

In Wintertimes of old when we were small,
Plump, pink, and loud, in dresses every one,
With our big albums that, alas, are gone,
How we saw the great wide world and owned it all!

Seated around the fire at nights in groups
We turned the pages — O how glad were we! —
Picture after picture, starry-eyed to see
The fine dragons galloping by in troops!

Then, I was among those happy ones, but now
With feet on fender and with bored, dull brow,
I, with a soul where still resentment seethes,

See, through a bright flame-album, march in view
My youth that like a passing soldier leaves
For life's black field, arms drawn, and bloody, too!

First Remorse

In those days when I wore a velvet suit,
My neck was covered by my curled brown hair
And, like full moons, my eyes were big and clear.
At dawn I left, bag on back, with laggard feet.

Always I plotted subterfuges on the route
To spite the jailers of my youthful jail;
For plums and apples then I tried to scale
The roadside walls guarding the orchard fruit.

So, far from boys and seats, I played it cool
One whole month to suit my wayward mood
Until one night I crept home fearfully

To find my mother crying with both lips glued
To the Cross! . . . O the burning shame in me!
Since then I have been always first at school.

My Mother

Sometimes on my head she lays her pure hands;
They are white, white as the linen's white strands.

She kisses my brow, speaks soft in my ear;
Her voice sounds gold through its worried care.

Her eyes colour the dreams I cannot define,
O poetry, ecstasy! O mother mine!

At the shrine of her feet weeping I fall,
A child still to her, although I am tall.

Before Two Portraits of My Mother

Painted in glad days when she was a lass,
My beloved mother in this portrait gleams
With lily-brow and look whose dazzle seems
Like light upon a bright Venetian glass!

In that, my mother is not what she was;
Her once-smooth brow is scored by time's deep
        fang,
And gone is the keen glow of days that sang
When her rose-poem marriage came to pass.

Today I compare, and am sad thereby,
This brow haloed by joy, and that by cares,
This sun-gold, that dimmed by sunset years.

But who can solve the heart's deep mystery!
Why do I smile when those sere lips I see?
At that smiling portrait why do I cry?

6

The Talisman

For the strife that evil days will soon afford
My mother gave me her picture as a stay;
This pledge I have honoured since that very day,
Fastened to my neck by a velvet cord.
"On your heart's altar (before death takes hold),
I shall be watching, child, on your behalf.
May this drive far off all licentious love
Like a church's guard, a votive lamp of gold."

Be calm within the gloom your grave embalms!
This sacred talisman of my youthful woe
Will keep your son intact from lewdness' arms.

So much I fear to see your picture wet
With tears from your soft eyes, then injured so,
That I would die of everlasting regret.

The Garden of Long Ago

Nothing is sweeter than coming back
    After long years with absence fraught,
        Than coming back
      On memory's flowered track
      To lilies without spot
        In childhood's garden plot

To the walled garden, sealed, the dumb, mute
    garden
      From which our fresh delights have fled,
        Our dumb, mute garden
      And the minuets then
      Our white-robed sisters led
        With green boughs overhead.

On April evenings, singing a glad song
　　Intermingled with choruses,
　　　　Singing a glad song,
　　　Proud-eyed they passed along
　　　Under waving trellises
　　　　Like the rhythm of verses

That came, all the same, from the villa's heart,
　　Soft low chords by an old lute made,
　　　　From the old villa's heart,
　　　To let us know, on our part,
　　　That near the shutters' shade
　　　　Some fair musician played.

It hurts the most for us to think again
　　Of things destroyed beyond our powers!
　　　　And oh, to think again
　　　When we come back with pain
　　　Through paths of faded flowers
　　　　To those young years of ours.

When we feel neurotic and agéd grown,
　　Unarmed, ill-used, and bruised by cares,
　　　　Morose and agéd grown,
　　　May, beyond oblivion,
　　　Youth's charms outlast the years
　　　　Although their price be tears!

Childhood Flight

Through old gardens, trampling the roses' peace,
To the pure threshold of yesterday's house
Like two sad, erring ghosts we come back now.

Let us reach the Past's dim strands that in stress
Of joy soon die. But all the same, see how
They stand, majestic in their ghostly dress.

Here let us plumb our hearts embossed with care.
Under the huge black tree-trunks bended low
That churl, Regret, is our mysterious host.

Let us follow, in a twenty-year-old ship,
Far-off, through private evenings gone and lost,
Our Childhood's flight back to its ideal slip.

Ruins

Sometimes I hear loud voices from the past
And see again my villaed infancy;
I find once more all things that belonged to me
When through the blinds the evening's light was
        cast.

Then in my soul suddenly my sight falls
On my blonde sisters grouped before the fire;
Around them the cat prowls, its spine held higher
In astonishment, watching them dress their dolls.

Ah! the calm of days forever beautiful
Whose radiant torches forever now are dead
And only gleam as flames in phantasy!

Now all's defunct, beneath a coffin-lid;
And under the tools of Grief's black masonry,
Like walls of brick, our joys are doomed to fall!

Evening Bells

Lost in the calm pride of the tall red hills
I roamed the swamps beyond my native grounds
When, in the East wind, and with sad, slow sounds
Angels in the evening shook the bells.

Like a shepherd-poet with a heart that swells,
In the roses' scent I breathed in their prayer,
While all my gathered anguish rambled there
Through dying golds along the myrtle dells.

So, when through this life I wander alone,
I keep in my mind a nook of the old soil
And that bright evening landscape seen once again;

While you, my heart, recall in your private fen
That Angelus of old, now faint, now still:
All those bronze birds from their own chapel
      flown!

On the Road

In your rosy solitudes, you yourself see
      Dazzling regrets like an ancient sun,
All the harm done to the park's wizardry
Where are plucked, in time to night's soft melody,
      Dead camellia blooms and roses wan.

Let us visit the faun with his frail flute
      Near the basins emitting vast sighs,
And the bench where, at eve, like a young poet,
I came, celebrating on my nimble lute
      The bright beams of your sapphire eyes.

Night embraces the lawn, to peace death-led,
      Weaving our grief into shadow-browns,
Weaving our ennui, our troubled dread,
My heart, so restless that it could be said
      You fear the phantoms of former moons!

Let us seek the broad slant road's mysterious
      bourne;
      There perhaps when our dear friends call
The kind fates will sadly raise their brows and turn
From childhood's tomb where their relics mourn
      In all our sleeping years' recoil.

The Muse's Cradle

From childhood's cot I made its very twin
Where my Muse sleeps and singing birds begin,
My white-robed Muse I'd give my all to win!

Listen to our kisses gold the warm Eves through . . .
But hush! Now at our door I hear that shrew,
Distress, and the sharp crunch of her black shoe!

Elite Loves

The Poet's Dream

Sometimes I want a sister good and sweet,
An angel-sister with a modest smile;
A sister who will put me in the style
To pray the way I ought, to hope, to wait.

I want a sister for life's timeless state,
One who in Art's great realm will share my ways
And shield me with the heaven of her gaze
When by the lamp she finds me sitting late.

Sometimes she will take my hands between her
        own
And whisper me good counsel in a tone
That the winged charm of music can assume;

And for her I shall grow, if I find fame,
A whole garden of lily and sunflower bloom
In a sky-blue poem addressed to her name.

Innocent Caprice

Winter, with his frost brush, paints on the windows
Pastels of gardens and roses in ice.
His cold stings to the quick, consigns to the house
My lady and her canaries and jockos.

But the little minx in her coach takes the air,
A furry ghost in a mantle of white,
Braving bad weather and bitter frost-bite;
More than one, seeing her go, still dreams of her.

Her two horses are white, her carriage is, too,
Driven abreast by a cockney cold as he sits;
In the snow their hoofs make round holes and pits,
And the night sky pales with a powdery hue.

To me as she passes, she turns her eyes' allure.
In order to complete the purity
Of that white ensemble, that make-believe
    bouquet,
I toss my heart to her on her coach's floor.

Petition

Queen, do you agree that a clasp can uncurl
The hair's bright waves with the teeth of its comb
So that I may take from it a small bit home
Of birdsong, love-nights born of your eyes' bright
    pearl?

Inside your heart's grove as the blackbirds skirl
A reedy flute gives rhythm to your soul's psalm.
Queen, do you agree that a clasp can uncurl
The hair's bright waves with the teeth of its comb?

A silk flower scented with rose, lily, beryl
To you I shall restore, sealed like a tomb
(Was this in Eden?) when we shall take ship home
On an ideal sea that lets no storms unfurl.

Queen, do you agree that a clasp can uncurl?

The Robin in the Woods

We were reading Werther in the deep woods where
Yesterday a robin sang in boughs above,
And I grasped your white hands, spoke to you of
    love
As I had spoken other times before.

But of my words and tone you took no care,
Dumb to the urging of a frank young man;
Then, rising, you through periwinkles ran
And, deep moved, you called me, crying out:
    "Look here!"

What had fallen from green leaves quivering
Was a suffering bird, stricken though young
That would soon be dead, poor soul of the Spring.

And you wept for it, regretting its song,
While I thought, staring at the deep blue sky,
Robin and love have found the same time to die.

Love's May

See how the Spring grows green and plenty
When the days ring blithe and twenty,
    Fol de dol day and tra la la,
See how at last the age is on me
When rags and tatters don't become me.
To a nice man this is not funny

O

tra la la
Young girls now good dispositions have,
Give us all the May for making love,
    Fol de dol day and tra la la.

14

Be blondes, brunettes, or be redheads, too,
Have eyes of any distant hue,
        Fol de dol day and tra la la,
Blue as asters, bright as beaded pearls,
But never a voice that whines or snarls,
You must be bright and jolly girls,

O

tra la la.
Now let our hearts beat high with mirth,
Full of all the blushing joys of earth,
        Fol de dol day and tra la la.

As for me, I have dreamed of it all,
Sad at heart amid the festival,
        Fol de dol day and tra la la,
Like a cold woods bird before the snow
Or the slow notes of an old oboe,
Sad at heart, I shall have to be so.

O

tra la la.
Sad as a hand when it waves good-bye
And pure as the light in God's great eye,
        Fol de dol day and tra la la.

See how enters the new love of May,
Let us live it quick and keep our hearts gay,
        Fol de dol day and tra la la,
For the bad days will happen too fast
And your singing be ended and past
In the grave where all must go at last.

O

tra la la
Beauties of twenty with hearts of gold,

Love sleeps too soon, as we have been told,
Fol de dol day and tra la la.

The Dead Beauty

Ah! at rest the dead beauty lies . . .
An angel moved her to paradise.

She sleeps amid the blue star-flowers,
As in a church through sabbath hours.

Ash-grey is the colour of her hair.
They have laid her in a coffin there.

Her green eyes that proclaim Death as liar
Will bear to her grave the moon's white fire.

Sentimental Theme

One eve I saw you smile at me
Upon the planet pastoral;
Lightly you dropped to the doorsill
Of my castle of porphyry.

And your eye was a diamond rare
That made the starry realms look pale.
Since then, girl, through hill or dale,
Girl, like Carrara marble fair,

Your voice now haunts me with its spell
And martyrs me to mystery;
Forever still your smile I see
Upon the planet pastoral.

Immaculate Love

I know a church with a pane of fine glass
Where angels led a master-hand to paint
In his own mystic style a blue-eyed saint
With star-haloed head, wearing a fringed dress.

Each night, soul-haunted by the heavenly press
Of echoed airs and nebulous dreams
I pray to her beneath the yellow gleams
Of a moon shining through each radiant tress.

In the same way, on my heart's pane I drew
That pale fair saint, my own romantic you,
My true love now and for all time to come.

But you remain unmoved, too proud, and, dumb,
Delight in watching as, dejected, low,
I roam through love as through a grave-yard now!

A Dead-Woman's Missal

This ivory missal
That you have given me
Is like a faded lily
A black page holds in thrall.

O outgoing legacy
From memory's recall,
Since you have given me
This ivory missal,

In it, outmoded, all
The cherished past of glory
Survives, shut up in me.
What a sprinkler for a pall,

This ivory missal!

Castles in Spain

In dreams I march, a conqueror bold,
Planting my flag where triumphal banners wave,
Full of wild pride, and notoriously brave,
To storm a town towered in bronze and gold.

A royal bird, vulture, condor, eagle old,
In dreams I soar to the sky-god's eyrie,
Scorching near the sun my twin-winged glory
All the wealth of heaven to grasp and hold.

But I'm no hospodar, no bird of prey.
Scarcely now can I the bitter fight endure
With vicious angels that my heart annoy;

And my proud dreams? Like wax they melt away
Before that hundred-walled eternal Troy,
Love's own city, by Virgins kept secure!

A Dead-Woman's Church

The old church doors are fastened tight;
I tamp the tiles with cautious feet
As they echo my own regret
For one sweet era lost from sight.

Beloved, I summon you tonight,
In love with your strange attraction!
And now the church the look takes on
Of your soul which it has swallowed quite.

Your body blooms on the lone altar,
And the sad nave is a winding sheet
Whose total glory wraps you there;

For me, your great eyes in the window
Will make this graveyard come alight
With soft mysterious candle-glow.

Cruel Beauty

Truly, but one love in the world should be found,
Only one love, fantastic though it be;
And I who seek its keen nobility
See how there is in my soul a deep wound.

She is proud and lovely, I am plain and shy.
I can approach her only in my dreams.
Poor wretch! The more I try, the higher she seems
And scorns my heart to woo her pleasing eye.

But see now, how capricious is Fate's reign!
If we two could exchange each other's faces
Her love for me would never have an equal!

And I would follow her, like a Spanish fool,
Either to fog-bound lands or sunny places,
Had heaven made me handsome and her plain!

With Feet on the Fender

Walled-in Dreams

Walled in by sadness let us dwell
In the warm moist chill of chambers
Where flower pots of old Septembers
Emit a reliquary smell.

Your tresses call to mind the ambers
Beneath that christian maiden's veils
In the basilica's old oils
On the carnal wealth of your members.

You flash your laugh's enamelled glaze
Onto a bright and scarlet jewel case
Inlaid with the boredom of my days.

Ah! May you, toward hope's sky of calm,
Make my heart, crystallized by ice,
Surge up like a tall and splendid palm!

Winter Evening

Ah! how the snow falls free!
My pane is a frosty garden now.
Ah! how the snow falls free!
What is life's spasm anyhow
To the sorrow in me, in me!

20

All the pools around lie icy.
My heart is dark. Where go? Where stay?
All the hopes around lie icy.
Now I am a new Norway,
Its fair skies are gone from me.

Cry, birds in February,
For the dire chill that fate disposes,
Cry, birds in February,
Cry for my ruins, cry for my roses,
In the boughs of a Juniper tree.

Ah! how the snow falls free!
My pane is a frosty garden now.
Ah! how the snow falls free!
What is life's spasm anyhow
To all the anxiousness in me! . . .

Five O'Clock

How sad Liszt sounds on a nearby piano!
. . . .
Upon the boudoir pane a frost-carver falls,
Etching strange vases, jewels that would have
      made
Cellini proud, a jumble, wind-disarrayed,
Distracting our peering eyes with crazy squalls.

How sad Haydn sounds on a nearby piano!
. . . .
Do not go out! Would you defy the squalls,
Beating cold sidewalks by winter disarrayed?
Stay! I shall have such gold as Cellini made,
Starry rings whose flash on fingers dear enthralls.

How sad Mozart sounds on a nearby piano!
. . . .
Five o'clock dies in a mute C crescendo.
— What is it? Your dear eyes are tear-pearled.
— It's because I see the young birds' hopes death-
    hurled
When the ice has frozen the fountains flow.

                    . . . sol, la, si, do.
— Gretchen, pour the tea in your cups from
    Yeddo.

For Ignace Paderewski

Master, when from your magic fingers I hear
That great Nocturne vibrate in golden bars;
When I hear its voice rise, fragrant with stars,
In an awakening, resonant and clear;

I think, as seraphic rhythms reappear
Under the wondrous blaze of some blue star,
That in you the great swan-song tubercular
Flies by, returned to life from slumber drear.

For you knew how to reanimate as well
His mighty instrument, and to his your heart
Is joined most strangely in its secret part.

Be proud, Paderewski, of the divine art
Heaven gave you, that wherever poets dwell
You can make the soul of Chopin cast a spell!

Gretchen the Pale

Hers is the beauty of a Rubens contour,
The same calm majesty to her belongs.

Her voice is golden as a lute when songs
On Venetian balconies their slow rhythms pour.

Her blonde hair, in a cascading shower,
Covers her virgin flesh like a mantel drawn;
Her step, a milk-white sigh of cool chiffon,
Could be an angel's tread at the vesper hour.

Her fair hair is like strange gold. Is she away
From Eden or from Erebus? Is she
Angel, this uncanny jewel of clay?

See her standing there, body like a young tree.
A willing Venus . . . Beware her demon charms!
She is that Pharos who slays with marble arms!

Odd Song

In rice shakos, with dark musketry,
Old of the old, the helmeted,
The tall roofs, winter-blanketed,
Extend their passports Paris-way.

The spectres on the promenade
Step lively by in crowds of grey.
In inward fullness let us stay
Like that, blind and with no words said . . .

May the guitar sleep inertly;
Gretchen, let no other dream impose
On the mad rapture I am in.

I would like to gather one by one
In the clear moonlight of your eye
Your every sweet Westphalian rose.

The Parlour

Over all the furnishings the dust holds sway,
The Venetian mirrors have shed their charm;
There lingers still, like old Parmese perfume,
The bitter sweetness of a long-known sachet.

And never more across the silence flow
Piano tunes in a rhythmic lullaby;
Mozart and Mendelssohn, wed in sweet harmony,
Are but heard in dreams in sleepy evening's glow.

But the poet, wandering in gross ennui,
Opening windows to the night's clear force,
Alone, fists clenched, and with the wildest glance

Suddenly imagines, haunted by remorse,
A solemn great ball, evolved from fantasy,
Where he thought he saw his dead parents dance.

The Shattered Violin

While your bow sobbed so blessedly
It shattered, filled with sadness,
On the night when you played, countess,
A theme from Paganini.

How all things fall through eagerness!
My love held infinity
On that night when you played, countess,
A theme from Paganini.

The violin sleeps in a narrow case
Polished in its carpentry
Since that night when, blonde hostess,
You played Paganini.

My heart rests in a pit of sadness
For love gone utterly.
It shattered on that night, countess,
When you played Paganini.

Roundel to My Pipe

With feet warm on the fender-sill,
Before a Bock, let's dream, my pipe,
Smoke-dreams of a congenial type,
This Winter eve, together still.

Since heaven holds me in its gripe
(Have I not suffered enough ill?)
With feet upon the fender-sill,
Before a Bock, let's dream, my pipe.

Soon death, whose coming now is ripe,
Will haul me far from out this hell
To the one which Satan runs so well.
We'll smoke in that place, too, my pipe,

With feet warm on the fender-sill.

Chopin

With the white blur of fingers sure
Do mourn again, O my mistress,
That march whose musical caress
Gave ecstasy to kings of yore.

Under the lights with their cold allure
Bestow on this heart sad eagerness
Through nights of dismal laziness
Sunk in your Hungarian boudoir.

May your piano throb and moan, and
May I forget with you an hour
In an Eden no one can see . . .

Play a bit, that I may understand
That soul in the dark notes whose power
Made a sick man, a mad man of me.

Sentimental Winter

Far windows! Limpid eyes whose looks I drain
Unsoiled by any gaze of commoner.
With Norway ice the fields like metal are;
May Winter's chill warm up our hearts again.

Like troops mourning the wrecks of Theban war,
Let us, my pet, treat our rancours tenderly
And, scorning life with its songs of sophistry,
Let good Death lead us down to Hades' door.

You will visit us like an icy spectre;
We shall not be old, but weary of life's faults;
Come, Death, take us on such an afternoon,

Languid on the divan, lulled by her guitar,
Whose dreamy motifs and whose muffled tune
Keep time to our ennui on the hellward waltz!

Farewell Violin

The night you played Mendelssohn, the flames
    there
Danced on the bright hearth; while in the salon
In long waves, a lamp-shade blended and made
    one
Its dreamy light and the chestnut of your hair.

Sad as a thrilling rumour of blossoms sere
Strewn on the valley's vesperal wind, the thin
High notes came sobbing from your violin;
In my heart each bow-stroke cast a bigger tear.

Then, before it grew late, I left the room
To rove till dawn, saddened, distraught, alone,
Confessing my young woes to the mystic moon;

I felt arise in me like dark perfume
That farewell music which under earth did seal
Both my love-dream and my dead hopes as well.

Mazurka

No charm enchants like this particular one,
Music wherein my languor is adored
On eves when I pursue the bronze light-beams
    poured
On the green rug of the well-known salon.

How I love to hear, by strange sorrow drawn,
Piano notes rising like a mandolin,
A sleepy rhythm where my despairs draw in
Their death-throes' scent and seek oblivion.

Swing open gloomy wide, you mental pit;
Despite the joy I draw from your dark sorrow
Rest from forgetting I can still there borrow

If my soul is drowned in the strange gamut
Of that sad tune Chopin has polished and caught,
Its broken rhythms by dark angels taught.

Winter-Chill

The gas-jets are almost closed now:
Warm my heart whose sobs of sorrow
Into your heart-beats overflow,
    Gretchen!

As it speaks sad things to you alone,
My nerves' harpsichord now takes its tone
From the early roses' rhythmic moan,
    Gretchen!

Take hold my hands, take hold my brow.
You are my dream, my Eldorado,
To which my youthful pathways go,
    Gretchen!

When the ice that is here to stay
Is joined in a wintery way
To the old mirrors of Venice' day,
    Gretchen!

When our two Persian cats, sleek, obese,
Display a calm inquiring gaze
As the flames purr in the fire-place,
    Gretchen!

When to you in the vigil's chill
Is thrust my inconsolable soul
In a tenderness beyond control,
    Gretchen!

Warm my heart, whose sobs of sorrow
Into your heart-beats overflow.
The gas-jets are nearly closed now . . .
    Gretchen!

28

October Evenings

— Yes, I suffer, these nights, sad devils, dear
        saints.
— One is always so suspected by Toussaints.
— My soul becomes a dune of sad memories.
— Ah! give me your brow, let me calm your crises.

— What do you want? Such am I in a city sense,
Sad man-about-town from the dress-circle flown,
One whose dream eludes, like a falcon,
The vile airs of the blockheads' affluence.

What do you want? Such am I . . . let me lie
        down
In idleness, in weariness, in a kiss,
A well-loved soul where moderate hopes can
        pass . . .

Behold this great galloping night, crimson
With rage, grand conqueror in solar wars,
Planting the triumpal flag of Octobers!

Virgilians

Autumn

How rich the heath is in that crimson-tinted time
When from the sky's dial-face has rung the vesper
chime!

How slow the oak-leaves fall before the ave-bell!
How sweet the sound from nearby chapels comes
as well!

Down there, great herds of mooing cows with
glaucous eyes
Amble, led by young lads to loud soliloquys.

In showers of grey the dust unfurls and then
declines,
Heavy with the musty heat of breezes and of vines.

In neighbouring solitudes all things are still;
The Sylphs have culled the dying perfume from
each bell.

How sad it is! October now is on the way!
Watteau, how I love you! Autran, O Millevoye!

Summer Night

A violin sighs its song of grief profound,
And a horn joins in, filling the calm night;

The Sylphides mourn, like souls in fearful plight,
And the tall yews' hearts emit a dying sound.

By a waking breeze each leaf to life is sped
And the light limbs sway in a rhythm free.
The song birds dream; under the milky eye
Of a Summer moon, my grief is harvested.
To the whispered concert by the crickets borne,
Those sabbath-seeking elves beneath the boughs,
In my pounding heart there echoes suddenly

The distant song of all night's majesty
Whose murmurs in the lazy heaven's drowse
Prolong until the rise of humid morn.

Watteau-Dream

When in the rusty gloaming the goatherds drove
Their great black bucks in time to the flutes' gold
    trills
Toward their native hamlet beyond the hills,
Returning through the fields where holly throve;

Wandering school boys, souls who hardly knew of
Trouble, still blameless during days without wrath,
Divorced from learning, down a husk-strewn
    wood path
Jesting we went, harkening to the rough

Roar of rapids in the valley where
Ran the yapping pup of the calm sons of Pan
Whose mournful piping fell on distant ears.

Then, weary, we lay down, chilled to the bone,
And sometimes, beaming, in our hay palace there
We feasted on the dawns and dined on stars.

Autumn Tarantella

Do you see, where the cattle gather,
The leaves fall on running water,
                    Running Water?

Do you see, on time's steep hillside,
My fallen illusions cut and dried,
                    All cut and dried?

With what a spate of angry floods
Blows the cold, sad wind of our moods,
                    Of my sad moods!

Do you see, where the cattle gather,
The leaves fall in running water,
                    Running water?

My October serenade at night
Swells upward to the moon's grand height
                    In the moon's clear light.

With what a spate of angry floods
Blows the cold, sad wind of our moods,
                    Of my sad moods!

The young dog frisks in the valley.
Let us follow the same alley,
                    That dull alley!

My October serenade at night
Swells upward to the moon's grand height,
                    In the moon's clear light.

One could say that every tree makes dark
Divorce between its leaf and bark,
                    Its old withered bark.

Ah! see there on time's steep hillside
My fallen illusions cut and dried,
                    All cut and dried!

Almost A Shepherd

The breezes are murmuring like litanies
And the flute fades out in soft aphonies.

The great steers are back. They moo in the stable
And the piping hot soup gladdens the table.

Pray, O Pan! Let us now go to bed, my lamb,
May our pickaxe-weary arms at last grow calm.

To silk horizons moonlight ripples and sways:
O Slumber! Give me your kiss of many joys.

All is shut. Night. Silence . . . a dog yelps out
    back.
I bed down. But in my soul a dream has struck.

Yes, it is delightful, this: to be so free
Living almost as a shepherd. A memory

Thrills in me. Back there, in childhood, my life
    flowed
Like that, pure and enraptured, far from the
    crowd!

Sentimental Garden

There, at fall of night, we loitered at our ease,
While round us, beetles in winged armies
Dazzled us with gold under leaden skies.

Great crimson horses wandered in bloody herds
Through sky-fields, and I clutched, trembling
        beyond words,
Your fingers in my hands, a nest of white birds.
Now we two, smiling at the evening star,
Felt the bright gleams of hope rise up once more
In our souls, tight shut like a dungeon's door.

The crumbling old steps that the dead ivy owns
Told us of gone days singing in the stones
At the old house-gates our memory enthrones.

Then from the nearby chapel the harsh strokes
Of the Angelus rang; without breaking our yokes,
We went in the playing night under the oaks.

Trampling grass-tufts where wandering crickets
        are,
Invisible, in a great green ship, afar,
We dreamed of rising with the evening star.

The Birds

To Rusbrock's teaching goes
My heart that bleeds for those
Bathing amidst cruel woes,
        All helter-skelter;
And, loving you, I try
To raise that dream on high
Of using my heart's tie
        For your shelter.

There, wild birds, you will withstand
All threats the fates command,
And have your own safe strand
        And sheltered moats;

Doves, swallows, tame fleet things
On my sure hands like rings,
Birds with bright humming wings,
    O ruby-throats!

Surely you will there live on,
Fearing no frost-eve's frown
Where under a copper sun,
    That torch of gloom,
Oft-times in flocks you go
While winds too harshly blow
And find beneath the snow
    Your frozen tomb.

Shielded without respite
As against a weary weight
After I cease my fight,
    Limb-weary toil;
You, over the huge vault
Will guide me beyond doubt,
Knowing better the route
    To heaven's smile!

Violin of the Vilanelle

In the cool of a valley under the moon
Both a blonde-headed lass and a brown gossoon
To an oboe's sound or a fiddle's tune
    Dance dance the vilanelle.

The heath is drenched with a lovely incense.
Stir up the joy in the coal-fire intense,
Go to it gaily and leap beyond sense,
    Dance dance the vilanelle.

On a bench of oak there the old folk stay,
Their eyes following you with a tearful dismay
As, brushing by, you pass so blithe and gay . . .
    Dance dance the vilanelle.

Go to it gaily! Let the silvery moon
Dart on your brows its changed reflection;
Late in the night, in the style of Saint-Jean,
    Dance dance the vilanelle.

Shepherdess

You whom I loved beneath the hollies tall
On rustic Eves that free and easy were,
Shepherdess, rustic, too, in your manner,
What of those evenings do you recall?
You were at my window a guiding star
And a gold star among the hollies tall.

On rustic Eves that free and easy are
You whom I loved beneath the hollies tall,
Shepherdess, rustic, too, in your manner,
Where now in this world do your footsteps fall?
— You are a shadow at my window there
And a deep sadness among the hollies tall.

Funereal Etchings

Old Streets

What do the old streets say to you
     Of towns that have had their day? . . .
Among the dust-motes that accrue
     From all of their decay,
Dreaming of things gone from view,
What do the old streets say to you?

When late at night you take a stroll
     To pay them your homage:
"Even more than an old man's soul
     You are his image."
This they say, as the fog-mists roll,
When late at night you take a stroll.

"Like old and nightly passersby
     Who walk our walls along
In themselves they bear black urns on high
     From years of doing wrong,
And their regrets leave silently
Like old and nightly passersby."

This is what in all towns where
     Many an old street stood

Is told among the dust-motes there
     Of things that have accrued
Among your glories gone for good,
O sad and dead towns that were!

Autumn Evenings

See how here the tulip there the rose,
By a group of bronze and marble statuaries,
In the park where love frolics under trees,
Sing through my nights, pink and monotonous.

The flowerbeds sang at eve in joyful chords
Where the moonlight's dance is a shifting show,
And where, sultry and sad, their high notes go,
Troubling the pure dreams of solitary birds.

See how here the tulip there the rose
And crystal lilies, crimson in twilight,
Radiate sadly to the sun in flight
That bears away from beasts and things their woes.

And my ravaged love, like bleeding flesh, makes
     whole
Its wounds and lets its madness find repose.
See how the lily, tulip, and the rose
Weep for the memories that wash my soul.

The Crows

In my heart I saw a flock of crows in flight,
Crowding that inner fen in gloomy bands,
Great crows from peaks renowned in many lands
They flew by in the moon's and torches' light.

Like a circle over graves, a dismal sight,
That has a zebra carrion-feast discovered,
In the ice-cold of my bones they hovered,
Waving in their beaks shredded hunks of meat.

Now, this prey ripened for these night-devils' yield
Was merely my tattered life where ever still
Vast ennuis arrived, converging on it,

Pitiless, tearing with great pecks of every bill
My soul, a carcass strewn on the daily field,
That these old crows will devour bit by bit.

The Hearse

Through foggy weather with cold wind and rain,
When the sky's blue robe must bear a sooty stain,
Late afternoon, on devils' holiday,
How sad it is to see a hearse go by,
Drawn by a team of dismal nags, in Fall,
Descending down a bumpy road and dull
Toward some grey-stone graveyard hid from view
That, like a tall corpse, lies prostrated too!
We bless ourselves and pause to hear the bell
That slowly rings the sad approach to tell
Of death's long afternoon we dreamed of so.
And then we think we see, as our steps slow,
Through gardens mildewed with all their dead
      leaves,
As at our doors the wind rustles our wreaths,
Leaving our homes, like hearts at a funeral,
Our own corpses in their coffins as well.

The Parrot

In days when her old age seemed hard
A poor negress kept as ward
That gay and lively bird.

Nestled in a tumbledown
Ugly shack right out of town,
They lived, the two alone.

It, as in old days at a fair,
Croaked for glory times that were,
Gripping her black shoulder there.

The old dame, intent, gave ear
Thinking the fine bird's words would bear
Her lover's soul right back to her.

For that bard, a fanciful man
With a cruel ironic plan,
To the credulous African

Had told that after he was gone
To death his soul would still live on
In his parrot's soul, known to none.

That is why the hag with her bald brow
When the evening light grew low
The deer-eyed bird would question so.

But it laughed at her, screeching mad
From morn to eve this Jeremiad:
"Ha! Ha! Gula! The loves I've had!"

That one scream was the death of her.
She thought that through the mindless burr
Of the bird, that blue-green chatterer,

The dead man wished, with mocking art,
To taunt the love of her old heart.
It killed her with its hateful smart.

The bird bemoaned her laid to rest,
Then made itself a stony nest
In an ancient wall impressed.

But it became as one ghost-wrung;
And when the night its song had sung
To skies unclouded, diamond-hung,

It could be said, seeing its distress,
The soul of that poor negress
Inside that bird wept tenderness.

A Grisly Banquet

A health to laughter! Madly I raise my cup
And drink like an art-student good at that game.
Laughter! Ha! ha! ha! It makes the eyes flame,
A gold ship gliding with love at the poop!

In vogue is the mirth of Jump-through-the-hoop.
Like jolly fat hunchbacks let's joke with the best;
May the clinking of crystal wake from their rest
Our fathers all heaped in a stone-bound group.

Clacking their old bones they come; for a gala meal
We have placed them seated round a circle,
A health to laughter and our skeletal sires!

Pour out the dark wine till it splashes and spills;
Poets, let us drink to Death in their skulls
To smother the sobs of our own angry fires.

Nocturnal Confession

Priest, I'm possessed. It's dark in the city,
A keep of sins, my soul is deadly black,
An awful grief pours onto the sidewalk
And from the abject herd no one comes to me.

All is calm. All sleep. A lonely city
From the gross horror of old manors is sick.
Priest, I'm possessed. It's dark in the city.
A keep of sins, my soul is deadly black.

In the park under the incivility
Of winter wind, Lucifer prowls to mock
My mad woe! . . . A suicide hones his knife-
    edge back.
It would be good to hang under this calm tree . . .
. . . .
Priest, pray for me. It's dark in the city.

The Negress' Tomb

After we fled the great wind of Winter,
Under the wan March skies, we took her down
To the dire copse, redolent of cinnamon,
Where the smells of all fresh shoots were in the air.

All kinds of birds dotted the high boughs there
With young heart-swells of sad song. In the moist
    grave
We brought her to, may the poor Negress have
Quiet sleep through months where green is
    everywhere!

The pious sun will cover up her pall,
And in his house of boughs, the good Bengalese
In youth will mourn a little her decease.

42

Perhaps when we come back some distant Spring,
From her heart, in some covert, we shall see a tall
Black lily among white roses blossoming.

The Coffin

On the day when a stroke seized my grandsire
By bad luck they had carried his coffin in;
Already the death-box was open to greet him
When his soul's candle suddenly caught fire.

And our souls from that horrible moment on
Respected that coffin's muted terror;
In the deep grave we imagined our grandsire
Haggard, self-devouring inside that mad prison.

So, when one died, the father, brother, stunned,
In the forbidden box refused to put his skin,
And the coffin, the accursed room within,
Remained, laden with shadow, mute and shunned.

For a long time I was not let discern
Or lay hands on that object which haunts my
        mood . . .
But since, sad wanderer in a wretched wood
Where each man is a trunk blazing my concern,

In my bizarre taste for the tomb I've grown so
Full of disdain for earth's noises and man;
In love with mystery like a great black swan
That sees by the light of a lunar flambeau.

Tonight I wished to see the coffin again
That has troubled me from my earliest year;
Assailing with a key its old-fashioned door,
Fearless, I entered the room of grief and pain.

43

For a long time there I stayed, before all
The box's gruesome horror, with a madman's gaze;
And I felt, gliding over my damp face,
Familiar shudders of a trapped animal.

With no qualms I stooped to swing its lid ajar,
Kissed its oak brow as I would a brother's brow;
And, gnawed by a morbid glad desire now,
I hoped that heaven would make of it my bier.

A Small Chapel

for Serge Usène

The Chapel in the Woods

We stood, two children pale and wan,
Before the fringed great altars where
Blessed Mary and her angels there
Among chrysanthemums smiled on.

Evening dusted through the empty nave;
Its yellow rays with darting slant
Stroked like a flower the pale tall saint
Who stood, like an icon stiff and grave.

And there we, two sad children, drank
The sanctuary's peaceful brew
Under a vigil lamp that threw
Amethystian waves which rose and sank.

Then our voices sailed, with joyous tones,
In one pure supplicating swell
That, like the peal of a sabbath bell,
Dim in the distance prays and moans . . .

Then we left . . . I remember well!
The forest slept in the moonlight
Where from the balm of summer night
Came the peal of a small chapel-bell . . .

Saint Cecilia

A beautiful saint in the skies
Leads the angelic orchestra
In that far-off basilica
Whose splendour haunts my eager eyes.

Since the Virgin of biblic days
Bequeathed this pious post to her,
A beautiful saint in the skies
Leads the angelic orchestra.

Far from this world's demonic guise
When mystery stalks the evening air,
May I in realms celestial hear
Your harpsichord's low mournful sighs,

My beautiful saint in the skies.

A Ticket to Heaven

Full of strange dreams and homesick melancholy,
I left one night for the saint's dear-loved home
Where was playing, in the Empyrean room,
An angel concert at heaven's feast on high.

Wearing a fringed tunic, I chanced to come,
Since no one kept watch over the entry,
Where they sang one night at the saint's dear-loved
      home,
Full of strange dreams and homesick melancholy.

Great dames in orange robes swept down the way;
Celestial servants wore liveries handsome;
Nor to my request was Cecilia dumb;
With her divine fingers I heard her play,

Full of strange dreams and homesick melancholy!

Hospital-Night Dream

Cecilia wore white, as in those oils of hers
Where the saint appears, a halo round her hair.
Jesus, Mary, and Joseph all were seated there;
And I listened, erect near the bannisters.

To the mysterious blaze of chandeliers
A strange and rhythmic music sudden roared
That her harp embellished in a quick accord . . .
Earthly music, oh, cease your churlish cheers!

No more I desire to enjoy, nor to sin;
The saint has told me that to hear her again
I have to leave earth's salvation behind.

And I want to return for the next soirée
That she will give in her planetary land
When angels tear me from this infirmary.

The Black Cloister

They walk in time to their sandals' muffled tread,
Head down, each stroking a great rosary,
And the blood-reflection of the evening sky
On the bleak splendour of the tiles burns red.

They vanish soon, as through dark mazes led,
Down aisles to crimson stages where earth-sin
Is quite held back and kept from coming in
By great angels etched on windows overhead.

Gloomy is their mien, and in their calm eyes
Like vast horizons of oceanic skies
Their habitual sternness burns cold and clear.

A heavenly light fills their ample mood,
For triumphant hope furrows the solitude
Of every silent ghost of Jesus here.

Communicants

Calm in the flowered church they file by me
Down the aisles and I follow them with my eyes,
Joining my pious hands in religious guise,
Full of keen-regret for by-gone ecstasy.

At the meal sent from heaven mysteriously
See how together all are kneeling now
Before an altar filled with lights that glow
Beside a wreath of spotless purity.

Their seraph fervour seemed to end so slow
That even as I watched them come back once more
From love-feast amid celestial fare,

I thought them ready then to fly, as though,
Under the haloes they so proudly bore,
Angels had placed gold wings upon them there.

The Deicides

I

The Jews, who in ancient times the prophets slew,
Were there when on the cross Christ died in blood;
Scoffers and hangmen they together stood
As Zion's crimes their celebrations drew.

Now see how under the stormy winds that blew
The Veil was uprooted from the walls' high state.
The Damned took flight; one could have said their
     weight

Of godly work on their heads came tumbling, too.

Since then, o'er all the earth, like stray dogs in
　　　flight,
They go, hordes of the damned; their race's blight
Is ever bound to bear remorse's load,

Finding everywhere along their bitter road
Scorn for pity, ghetto for fatherland,
Affront for alms, when they lift a begging hand.

II

Others there are, vile hordes encased in grime,
Crushing the Lord beneath defiance' weight
When He to them extends from His cross's height
His great bronze arms in exordia sublime.

Spewing discordant spite like dread quicklime,
Spitting a curse on Bread that for them You made,
They pass. Now these, who are called Your sons,
　　　my God,
Flog You with strong symbolic strokes through
　　　time.

Somewhere, exiled to eternal horror,
In lamenting throngs, these vile wretches will flee,
Mad with shame, into dark nights of blasphemy

While on their brows, standing out mysteriously,
Will gleam, like a badge of dire torture
Etched in blood, the victim's eternal scar.

The Monk's Death

Behold how sad the brothers come
To the cell where your body lies.

Your soul is full of anguished cries
And airs with dreary notes and glum.

Bring him now the Viaticum.
Saint Benedict, help his death along!
Though he is weak, make him be strong,
Shielded by your old saint's wisdom.

So be it now in God's great heart.
Clement, give a laughing good-bye
As you leave this world's impure tie.

Go now, return to your hope's first start.
May the bronze monastery bell toll
Tonight on its way your skyward soul!

Diptych

I know a Flemish diptych displayed
Inside an ancient chapel here
Where Jesus, his blessed mother near,
Digs up the sand with a tiny spade.

Not painted by Rubens or Memling,
But worthy of their galleries;
The Virgin in white draperies
At a white wheel is busily spinning.

The spade, coloured like tart wine,
In God's thin hands gleams at its toil;
The sunlight burns a red farewell
Down there, toward the holy Zion.

The young child before the shanty
That Nazareth's carpenter has
Piles up a heap that could be the base
Of a grim hill in times to be.

Jesus gets dirty at His play.
His fingers are spotted with soil;
On each cheek the marks of his toil
Are set like gleams of a pale ray.

What stern task so precociously
Does Jesus Christ there labour at?
Is he laying down in spirit
The base of a future Calvary?

The Ruined Chapel

I come back, raw with cold, in the drizzle's wake,
Through an October park's wild and messy plight.
At the street-end, a tall Jesus stands upright
Among debris that a ruined chapel make.

Among bugloss and viburnum there I rake,
Dreaming, the old soil where an owl reposes, too.
The maple bends in the wind like bamboo,
And in my breast I feel my poor heart break.

Bells of dead ages ring out their rhythms black,
All the sadnesses of gold, the hopeless glooms,
Borne by an odour that the dream brings back;

Ah! how, knees frozen to an old portal,
I mourn the ruin of that tiny chapel . . .
On the shattered wall! A stained-glass splinter
    blooms!

Reply from the Cross

What grief, O Christ, engulfed Your soul's sad fate
When on Golgotha's tree your body died?
Was it to leave your Marys, and more beside,

At that rock where Your cross was planted
     straight.

When the grave choir without You mourned Your
     fate
And nails clenched Your hands; when on the
     broad heath
Your soul scattered the bloom of its breath,
Outspeeding Your flight to its heavenly state;

What great sob of sorrow's timeless throes
Did You exhale when, at the end of toil,
You at last prepared once more to gain Your goal?

Will You this inner mystery disclose?
"It was, young man, because, after the drunk gall,
I could not embrace my hangmen on earth's soil!"

Carmelites

In the cloister's shade they walk solemnly,
And their feet are cold rubbing on the tiles,
While the slow sad squeaking of their sandals
Rises like the song of their chastity.

To the seraphic flash of each stern eye
Their torches respond with the fitting scales;
In the cloister's cold they walk solemnly
And their feet make velvet music on the tiles.

One nun has returned to eternity
To forget at last all the world's scandals;
To her death-couch, deep in their maze of cells,
Her sister nuns repair. That is why

In their cloisters they have long marched solemnly.

52

Our Lady of the Snows

Our blessed Lady in a mantle fair
    From her flowery country
Each night descends to where Jesus slumbers there
    In his own Ville-Marie.
The Virgin strides beneath a torch of stars
    That triumphant angels bear
Marching in time to those unearthly bars
    That through high heaven roar.

Our blessed Lady had set her throne there,
    Upon our Mount Royal,
And from that height her eye subdues the satyr
    In his pit infernal.
For she has proclaimed: "Let an angel's arm
    Of fire watch over you,
My silver city collared in snow's white charm,"
    That Lady in sky-blue.

Our blessed Lady, save us at Your command
    From all but Your mild sway!
Drive far off the stranger! In this chill land
    Be You our strength and stay.
This our request abloom with gilded things,
    May You with Your mild eyes
Peruse it when on rosy evenings
    You come to us from the skies.

Among small angels, our blessed Lady
    In grief has sorrowed long;
So much that in hidden heavens (they say)
    One hears an alien song.
And may our Virgin, bearing her own Eden,
    O the flowering She!
Bring to bloom in the very same garden
    Her France and her Ville-Marie!

Evening Prayers

When every sound inside the house was still
And my young sisters slept, fatigued, enthroned
In old arm-chairs that their dead grandsires
    owned,
And no sound broke that nameless inner thrill,

Down from her room my mother softly crept
To sit down before the black and white keys;
Music tinged with September vagaries
From her hands on trembling ivory swept.

I listened, heart full of care and regret,
And on the carpet let my dim eyes stray
Or, as the cinders split my reverie,
I lifted them to scan each portrait set.

And while all things were locked in slumber's
    balm,
And as sad notes rose to join the tick-tock
Intermittent click of the old German clock
That had been the only sound to break the calm,

Little by little night wrought to its will
Cinders, casements, screens; through such
    evenings
In spite of all the warmth a log-fire brings
How at our spines we felt a sudden chill!

The clock whispered midnight, mourning the dead
    lamp,
And my sisters woke to seek their beds at last,
With pale brows, dishevelled hair, and eyes
    downcast
Under drowsiness brushing their temples damp;

But in that room full of lunar harmonies
Before we rose to our night's rest again
There was a dull, taciturn wait, and then,
Sudden, the silver clash of rosaries . . .

And even as strange Liszt sonatas we heard
That slowly in our hearts made their retreat,
The family knelt in prayer to the beat,
Remote and clear, of the angel's harpsichord.

Pastels and Porcelains

Creole Fantasy

All crimson now the pink verandah clothes
To the soft mild lilt of a mandolin;
In evening reds, to the sweet scent of rose,
All crimson now the pink verandah clothes.

Amid gold streams on Egyptian vases
Under the balmy breeze, sweet smelling plants
Dissolve to blue and find their hidden haunts
Amid gold streams on Egyptian vases.

The birds get drunk on music's fragrant charms
As the skies continue their starry dance;
And Love goes by, held in the breezes arms,
The soul gets drunk on music's fragrant charms.

And crimson now the pink verandah clothes
As in her Louisianan paradise
Amid the stillness, to the sweet scent of rose,
In a rosy hammock the creole finds repose.

Touch-Me-Nots

In her ducal salon in a carved armchair,
In violet gauze, a Viennese aristocrat

Devoutly leafs, with fingers pale and flat,
Her vellum missal, wearing it threadbare.

She remembers, dreaming of music there,
That poor guitarist whose reflected gaze
Was bright with love of art, who near her
      bookcase
Had come to talk, smelling flowers in a jar.

The night lamp flickers, and the old clock rings;
Her book aside, Madame with a shuddering yawn
Regains her great silver bed, worthy of kings.

Tears wet her lashes . . . when dawn burned
      gold ingots
On proud heraldic doors, the book upon
The Magyar carpet showed dead touch-me-nots.
   . . .

Supper's King

Grave and bent, a tall negro scurries by,
In shining livery at a courier's pace;
The stuffed peacock rises, a wreath of smoking
      lace,
From the silver platter to the ceiling high.

The triumphal course in the covered buffet
Burns. The whole room is bathed in golden light;
At the massive table all the feast await
From great-uncle down to the child knee-high.

A sudden mirth breaks forth in fine relief.
The youngest, a rebellious lad, sinks down
Upon the table-cloth's best decoration.

They all applaud. Sambo swoons, holding his ribs,
While behind her fan, hiding her handkerchief,
Grandma dabs lightly both her white eyelids.

Tawny Landscape

On a high cliff where the horizon rose,
Stand the trees, like old men by rickets bent
Or damned souls under the whips of torment,
Twisting in despair their fantastic torsos.

It is Winter; it is Death; on Arctic snows,
Flogging their horses at a break-neck pace
To far-off camps where still their fires blaze,
The hunters ride, chill beneath their heavy clothes.

The north wind howls; it hails; night falls in gloom;
See how suddenly through the shadows loom
Savage packs of wolves, through starvation bold.

Stiff-legged they leap; in tawny swarms they rise,
And the stark horror of their burning eyes
Lights the white loneliness with sparks of gold.

Fan

In the old parlour with its faded lace
The Japan sofa's rich brocade is bright
With lilies gold, and all that chiffon white
Outlives its bygone ladies' ballroom grace.

But, O triumphant grief! Near the bronze griffin's
    base
An ancient ostrich plume is fraying quite,
In the old parlour with its faded lace
The Japan sofa's rich brocade is bright.

Sometimes, as time whirs in its frantic race,
The fan revives an old thrill, as if a light
Sudden touch of a dead woman's hands might
Mysteriously have risen from that place,

In the old parlour with its faded lace.

The Antique Dealer

Rolling a great ring as bony fingers part,
The old antique dealer, an Algerian Jew,
Goldsmith, jeweller, and good swordsmith, too,
Wanders, pauses, strays, deep in his own mart.

Then from iron lamps that feverishly start,
Throwing vague shadows near, this modern
        Shylock
Recoils in horror. Rigid as a block
He seems to suffer daggers in his heart.

Poor wretch! This old artist found out too late
That the royal ring, bought at an outrageous fee,
Was but a trinket, a fraud or fool's bait.

That is why, beneath the mirrored chandelier
His wild eyes veer and strain so horribly
While sparkling rubies cast their dreary glare.

Camellias

In the boudoir draped with Mechlin lace, tonight
Emmeline is at the ball, and all is still.

Only the camellias in a sea-green bowl
Languidly close their witching eyes from sight.

On scattered onyx, her rings and jewels throw
Gleams that strike upon the silver box's sheen.

All mourn the absent Fair with vague notes of woe.
An angry parrot digests his black spleen.

The clock chimes. It is dawn. And on the stair
A foot sounds with a thin hiss of satin gauze.

All things wake, heavy from nocturnal joys.
Her shoe's slight sound proclaims the Mistress
        there.

A fresh rose-bouquet her gentle hand now prunes;
Dawning tears veil her eyes and cast them down.

The ball has brought the first grief she has known.
Now her youth conjures the dire void of things

In front of pink camellias dead and gone.

Family Clock

Your brazen chimes are all done now:
Behold, you are stilled forever,
And the hours will vibrate never
In the huge parlour I loved so

When, after study, at night I went
To smoke and to creak rhythmic verse,
Where, sheltered from a world perverse,
Long, also lovely hours I spent.

On the buffet with its dark tones
Of oldest oak, O sombre clock,
Does your ghost mourn for an epoch
Of worried cares and dismal groans?

Could it be that a deadly grief
Has harried you like grim remorse,
You great timepiece, and stopped your course
After our ancestors found death?

A Dead-Woman's Shoe

All gold and grey, that fragile shoe
With its scented silken straps;
Between my hands tonight it sleeps
Like a mysterious cameo.

Just now I found it suddenly
Lying deep inside an old commode . . .
A shoe, small, in an ancient mode,
All hail, O shoe of memory! . . .

For, ever since, led by Chopin's lines,
She took her flesh and blood away
To sleep forever in a grey
Chill gloomy place beneath the pines,

Through every year I have remained,
Crushed beneath an iron load;
It makes a hell of the abode
In which my poor damned soul is chained.

And now, in that December vigil,
When all my heart was filled with gloom,
I found at the bottom of my room
A shoe her tender foot let fall.

It alone remains for me to view,
Its twin has found an angel home. . . .
. . . .
Now barefoot through the mud I roam. . . .
For my soul is a broken shoe.

An Old Romantic

Wrapped in a shawl and sheltered from the cold
In a window-seat near her pots of flowers,

Miss Adele sits at ease while her eye devours
A Dumas novel like a twenty-year-old.

A convent of antiquities behold
In her whose boudoir sprawls in one strange
        mound;
There engrained in her devout creed are found
Vases, onyx, pictures, all-sized books untold.

On a cushion an old Persian tomcat purrs
While the old dame squanders that heart of hers
And all its worries within a yellowed book.

But, trapped in her fond dream, she does not see
From the street peer in, with a mocking look,
A bragging organ-grinder from Barbary!

Old Cupboard

Sleep on, revered jumble of old porcelains,
All shut-up, all cold, as cold as dead men's eyes;
Japanese tea-sets that speak of other days
And the rich meals of lovely chatelaines!

Old wool's damp smell is what your wood retains
And the dread arising from frail gold things;
Your cups bespeak, upon the lips of kings,
Their Hebes, pastel pictures that clear light strains,

Old flower gardens where the blossoms last,
An arabesque with blue mice in its sky . . .
O tall dark wardrobe, relic of the past!

Yesterday, while setting your wooden door ajar,
I thought I saw pass in spectral memory
Hazy couples going to midnight supper.

Vase

There is a vase of Egypt chiselled fair
Where blue sphinx and amber lions live in paint:
In profile, one can see, supple, with back bent,
An immobile Isis twisting her hair.

Aflame, gold ships go gliding where no sails are
On a silver stream up to the sky's blue tint;
There is a vase of Egypt chiselled fair
Where blue sphinx and amber lions live in paint.

My soul's an ornate vase, with moulding faint,
Where old sad hopes all badly painted are;
Now my heart endures them like a burn-scar,
But death will botch them soon, and my
          complaint . . .

For my life is a vase not chiselled fair.

Tragic Vespers

Dismal Music

While dreaming of death and her absent boudoir
I feel fatigued in every bone of me;
Near my Persian cat, in my dark armchair,
I purge myself with exotic melody
Under chandeliers whose lights are prompt to pour
On the grave of sluggish dreams their sympathy.

I have always loved, full of silence now,
To live, closed in, in a flat's solemnity
Where my heart rings bells out of misery
And, plunged in horror, decides to follow,
Sad as a dead sound, closed as an old folio,
Those tunes vibrating like waves of the sea.

What do love and its dreams matter to me,
A plebian lacking artistic fame?
For, in a harpsichord's minor key,
I want to drown in existence' mournful calm
And see unfold my murderous ennui
In a prelude whose soul is symphonic balm.

I am one whose life is as a coffin shown
That only hideous songs of mutes can enter
Where my weary ghost, as if beneath its stone,

Late at night is talking to remorseful despair,
Calling in vain like so many ghosts well known
Who can only speak to a dead man's ear.

Under finger-rhythms soft and slow, go on.
Play those sad Chopinades with a dying fall.
How I hate this life with its dark carillon!
O griefs, let these sad aubades engulf you all
Or I'll hang tonight these parlour doors upon
In order to sing the red serenades of hell.

A dire instrument, you mock me, mad keyboard!
Softly, pianist, O let me dream once more!
More slowly, please! . . . My coffin is lowered
To the shock of irons, amid the grim decor
Of funereal fields where dead bones are poured,
And my heart moans like a horn's long uproar!

   . . .

The Coffin-Maker

Mr. Christian Loftel has no other trade
Than coffin-maker for his brothers all,
Mid funeral bills, deep inside a stall
Where for forty years a light has scarcely strayed.

No one comes, so great a gap his looks have made;
He bears the chill of funerary urns.
Sometimes a mourner seeks advice, then returns,
Mind-haunted whence that worried ghost has
    preyed.

O wise man, who always keeps your secrecy,
You know quite well, Mr. Christian Loftel,
What furrowed your brow and gave you your
    scowl.

Tell me! While planing each plank furiously
With your bumping tool, how many mortal souls
Have regaled you with their posthumous tales?

Sad Marches

In me I hear sad voices cry
Beyond the bounds of time and space
When noted march-bands drumming race
To tunes conceived in Germany.

And if I sob distractedly,
Mad-thrilled within my rib-cage space,
It is that I hear sad voices cry
Beyond the bounds of time and space.

Like ghostly zebras gliding by
My maddened visions strangely race
And I am so haunted in that place
That still, in the dark inside of me,

I hear sad voices groan and cry.

The Haunted Well

In the black well that you see there
Lie all the springs of drama here.
On the night wind a belling deer
In woodlands will the truth declare.

Here a mad lover, in days that were,
Through woman won a watery bier.
In the black well that you see there
Lie all the springs of drama here.

Psst! Don't come! A mysterious flare
Flames from a ghost on fire; we hear
A soul's last gasp all ghastly clear,
Like feast-sounds falling on night air

In the black well that you see there.

The Idiot Girl

I

She wished to find the Easter bells
Along the roads of many lands;
Where many evenings cast their spells
Her feet dropped blood upon the sands.
     Ah! fol derol day,
On her feet sharp stones have set their wheals.
They said, "Unlock your pocket's seals."
— "Nay, they're closer to the Roman strands:
I want to find the bells, the bells,
     I want to find the bells
And I will hold them in my hands."
Ah! fol derol lol derol day.

II

She went then at the vesper hour,
Alone in the wood at evening.
She dreamed of a cathedral tower
Whose bells in the belfry ring.
     Ah! fol derol day,
She dreamed of a cathedral tower,
Then all at once with mad shrill power
Her far-off voice rose, clamoring:
"I want to find the bells, the bells,
     I want to find the bells

And I will hold them in my hands."
Ah! fol derol lol derol day.

III

One dawn where the road winds through the hills
They found her by a ditch's side.
On the night that brought back the bells
The poor idiot girl had died.
     Ah! fol derol day.
On the night that brought back the bells
With the close-by clang of brazen peals
Her golden dream was justified:
An angel rang the bells, the bells;
     Oh high he put the bells;
He put them all between her hands.
Ah! fol derol lol derol day.

The Ghostly Ox

The great sea-green-hornéd ox all red
Down there is haunting the field's peace;
Mid the lying herd, mooing without cease,
He moves with bellows hoarse and dread.

Under a beech at night the flocks
Have made their merry noises cease.
The great sea-green-hornéd ox all red
Down there is haunting the field's peace.

Woe to the wicked wiles of a fox!
Cowboys in rags, belles in white lace,
Go head over heels as you race!
Through thorn-bush, meadow, over sharp rocks

Flee the red and sea-green-hornéd ox.

Tristia

The Lake

Remember, my heart, before the waves in flight
On that grave lake, under the evening's gold,
That unlucky pair whose dire bark rolled
Over, foundering with their love one night.

How all things fret and sob around about!
The wind drops star-tears on the reeds nearby;
And lilies are mirrored, like birds in the sky,
As if to find their images afloat.

But nothing has risen since that evening's harm
When, with their two lives twined, those lovers
    died,
And the still pools to the gold waterside
Say that they sleep well under their clear calm.

A vast and sleeping lake, man's lot behold,
Full, under the cold mask its waves assume,
Of drowned illusions and our fair dreams' doom,
Where hope reflects in vain its stars of gold.

Corregio's Last Angel

With haggard eyes and pallid cheek,
But with no regrets and heart untired,
In his poor Italian attic
The great Corregio expired.

The master's children and good wife
Around his death-bed's bitter smart
Try to put a little of his life
Back into his scarcely beating heart.

But it is the mind's own vision
That foments the body's fever,
And his soul in death's agitation
Rings out its harmony bizarre.

He wants to paint. With gentle ease
He rises up from off his pillow
Like some dreamy angel in a daze
Who for a time lets heaven go.

His eye searches all the room about,
Then freezes, astonished in its turn.
He sees his model, beyond all doubt,
In the cradle of his latest born.

His young child, the panel quite nearby,
Rosy in the orange linen's glow,
Had joined his hands angelically
To petition the Bambino.

And the tie of his filial prayer
To heaven's wish was made secure:
In a night of gold Italian air,
A vision of white radiance pure.

"Quick, bring me now a paint-brush, good!
My colours, too! the artist said,
"I want to paint the sad attitude
Of my child in his cradle-bed."

"My paint-brush," raved Corregio,
"I want in flight to grip and hold
All this sublime ideal of snow
Before it returns to heaven's gold!"

How he paints! On the canvas fair
In deep waves his genius pierces through!
That is a fair-haired angel there
Wearing a cloak of starry hue!

But the painter, seized by a stroke,
Soon dies on the spot where he falls
The while the sweat-beads on his neck
Become hardened into waxy pearls.

So this strange artist's life was done
Whose heart was full of his ideal;
Who made an angel out of his son
To make him an orphan as well.

Old Artist's Christmas

The door bangs and icy winds moan,
An angel bears the prize away.
Noel, on a housetop poor and grey,
Like a *De Profundis,* beats down.

With eyes glued to his unshaped stone
The artist died amid the fray.
The door bangs and icy winds moan,
An angel bears his prize away.

O Paradise! By his death you show
Your pity for his thorny way.
May he sleep, then, warm-clad alway,
His cot such freezing cold did know!

The door bangs and icy winds moan . . .

The Bell in the Mist

Hear, O hear, O my poor soul. There is a cry
Far-off in the fog! It is a bell all right!
Its notes chime through the dark of a chill night
And a great grief touches us before they die.

What think you now? What dreams are in your
    mind's eye?
You who pray no more. Ah! poor wretch, could
    it be
That you are comparing your difficulty
To a bell that dreams of Angeluses gone by? . . .

How it whines for you, monotoned and dismal,
How it tolls for you in autumn mist, a bell
That cries for some church consigned to night's
    dark reign,

Regretting with great strokes of ringing pain
The faithful ones who leave its shining wall,
As you regret your hopes' exile as well.

Christ on the Cross

That tall plaster Christ I gazed at passing by
Like an indulgence nailed to the old door
Of a convent, a lowering stage before
Which I would kneel in meek idolatry.

The other night, when crickets began to cry,
Roaming dim meadows, reciting prayer
Hymns to Apollo, god of art and war,
With wind-blown hair and blue-eyed reverie.

I saw, next to the ruins of a wall,
The great heap of a huge old cross, with all
Its crumpled plaster among primroses strewn,

And I stood there, with sad and thoughtful eyes,
Hearing in me heart-hammers driving home
The black nails of my own inmost Calvaries!

Lament

Like tears of gold leached from my heart's thin
        wall,
Leaves of my happiness, you fall, fall, fall.

You fall on dream-gardens whence I depart,
Hair stirred by the wind of each bad day's smart.

You fall, like shards from a pure inner tree,
Scattered around the alley's statuary.

Hues of former days, and child robes outworn,
When great winds in Autumn blow their hunting
        horn.

Always you fall, mingling your agonies,
You fall, faint, uniting your harmonies.

You have fallen on road ruts at sunrise;
You fall from my hands, you weep from my eyes.

Like tears of gold leached from my heart's thin
        wall,
In my twenty arid years you fall, fall, fall.

Empty Melancholy

Like deep void chasms are our hearts below,
My dear, we both feel pain; come, let us go.

Let us flee to Illusion's castle high,
And let us flee from Fact's bewitching eye.

On our twenty-year ship like dreams let's sail
To strands of Thule or to Delusion's isle.

In a golden land, full of birds and song,
On the reeds' fresh bed we shall sleep as one;

We shall rest at ease from disaster's jars
In the trill of flutes and the dance of stars.

Let us flee to Illusion's castle high,
And let us flee from Fact's bewitching eye.

Do you want to die, tell me? We both feel woe,
Like deep void chasms are our hearts below.

October Roses

So not to see the autumn roses fall,
Cloister your dead heart in my heart made dead.
Against sick evenings my grief is sped,
To the monotonous month a parallel.

Belated now, a glad crimson clashes all
Against the aching woodland's spotted red. . . .
So not to see the autumn roses fall,
Cloister your dead heart in my heart made dead.

And over there the cypresses look dull,
We are soon accustomed to their shade,

Underground is set a fresh and open bed;
There we two shall sleep, my beautiful,

So not to see the autumn roses fall.

My Christmas Clog

I

Jesus to you His glad presence brings,
His hands, children, are full of playthings.

On this same day, be sure to put
A new hat in the fire-place's grate.

And be good, do not cry at last . . .
Hush! hear his footsteps coming fast.

He has swung the big door open wide,
He comes, bringing good things inside.

Be happy, cherubs, whose bright heads glow
Like those by Rubens or Corregio.

Sleep well among your nappery
Or you will make the angels die.

Sleep, until the glad church bells chime
The hour of your wake-up time.

II

For us, strong sons of Bohemia,
How boredom makes Christmas anaemia!

For us Jesus no more descends,
We have had too many toys, my friends.

We have too much new-born grief to put
In our fire-place's infernal soot.

So much despair befouls our walk
That all our clogs with it are black.

Man by hunger dead and artists bare
Have but their sad hearts for goodies here.

Passer-By

I saw, veiled like a ghost whose grief we own,
In a large dark park a woman yesterday:
Funereal and strange, she went away,
Hiding her pride beneath a mask of stone.

In that clear evening I would not have known,
Save for one look, her restrained agony;
Then she disappeared into an alley
Dark as the grief that filled her heart alone.

My youth and that poor waif walk hand in hand;
Many will cross it in this path below
Where life will lead it harshly to the grave;

All will see it pass, a dry leaf in the flow
Of wind that eddies, falls, and fades at eve;
But none will love and none will understand.

Under the Fauns

We huddled silent, moved with haggard brow,
In flaming Junes of gold, daydreamers still,
Smelly, tired, deep-involved, and quick to feel,
Through fallen eves that in their triumphs glow.

Standing on grey steps against the chiaroscuro
Of rural trees with smells numbing the sense,
We found there great marble statues, immense,
Lying in sleeping pride, scattered out below.

Sometimes, deep-cloistered in old kiosks nearby
We heard the cries that bell-mad people make
Whose distant voices fall away and break,

And some vague feelings filled our hearts always
When before these dismal statues' stoney gaze,
Haggard we huddled, my doleful Grief and I.

Glooms

In my heart the thin mists of sadness cast
And the caw of its hidden crows conjoin;
And still I ponder on that ship gone down,
My twenty years in a starry sea now lost.

Oh, when can I, like a crucifix, put out
Between my fingers that peace so old and dear
Whose voice and music now I never hear
In the mess my groaning life is all about?

With all my soul long thoughts I fain would have,
Beneath the cypress of that corner grave
Where lie in icy tombs my childhood's charms.

I can no more; I feel funereal arms
Raise me to Reality, whose torchlit fumes
Embrace at dead of night my own strange glooms.

Song of Wine

Fresh in joy's live light all things coincide,
This fine May eve! Like living hopes that once
Were in my heart, the choiring birds announce
Their prelude to my window open wide.

O fine May eve! O happy eve of May!
A distant organ beats out frigid chords;

And long shafts of sun, like crimson swords,
Cut to the heart the scent of dying day.

How gay, how glad am I! Pour out, pour out
Once more the wine into the chiming glass
That I may lose the pain of days which pass
In scorn for all the wicked human rout.

How glad am I! My wine and art be blest!
I, too, have dreamed of making poetry
That lives, of poems which sound the exequy
For autumn winds that pass in far-off mist.

The bitter laugh of rage is now good form,
And I, a poet, must eat scorn for food.
I have a heart but am not understood
Except in moonlight and in great nights of storm.

Woman! I drink to you who mock the path
Where the rose-dream calls with arms flung wide;
I drink, too, to you, men with brows of pride,
Who first refuse my hand then scorn my life!

When the starry sky becomes one glorious roof,
And when a hymn resounds for golden Spring,
I do not weep for all the days' calm going,
Who wary grope within my own black youth.

How glad am I, May eve, all eves above.
Not drunk but desperately glad am I! . . .
Has living grown at last to be a joy?
Has my heart, too, been healed of my sick love?

The clocks have struck and the wind smells of
      night . . .
Now the wine gurgles as I pour it out.
So glad am I that as I laugh and shout
I fear I shall break down and sob outright.

78

Recovered Poems

Whimsical Dream

The brown proud oaks traced against the sad sky's
    hues
Dark outlines that to their own rhythms move;
The darkling elms and fine langourous yews
    Cast shadows on the green nests of love.

Here stand strange fountains and silk waterfalls;
Heart-shaped shrubs and silver Cupidons,
And, deep in the park between two long aisles,
    A deer, in Bonheur's style, of bronze.

Great-necked and handsome, the swans both black
    and white
On the moss and in the waters frisk and play;
Near the golden nymphs, to the mild moon's
    height,
    In handsome flocks the wild birds fly.

Soft and distinct sounds, weak in far-off space,
Echo harmoniously through the cool air;
The cloudy night with languid dreams comes to
    place
    Its gulf of darkness everywhere.

To a violin's sob and echo again
Wakes the voice of one who is not with me yet;
My soul, quick-reminded of memory's pain,
    Is drowned in another regret.

How sweet to end our souls' afflictions dire,
When time weighs down on us like fierce remorse,
— Whether despair or a black thought require —
    How sweet it is to end life's course!

I still recall . . . through one May night I went,
Blending my mood to the song the hot winds sing;
Then I heard, beating beyond the embankment,
    A black Bucephalus galloping.

With these vague charming sounds, fantastically
My romantic dream returned to its void;
And in the park where sudden fresh airs play
    Amid the old picturesque deployed,

Alone, the pale oaks trace in the sad sky's hues
Less sombre lines that to their rhythms move;
The darkling elms and the quivering yews
    Cast shadows on the nests of love!

Sylvio Mourns

Only a poor mean wretch am I:
My mother left when I was small;
Sick and morbid I wander by,
On earth I have no friends at all.

For my stay and sole companion —
On madcap days it gained me bread —
I have but a poor violin;
And willow shade for my only bed.

My heart is like the heavens, wide;
And though my eyes reveal no flame,
I read in life a happy tide
That I must search my soul to claim.

I stay awake on moonlight eves
And play my sad and ancient airs
That charm the nightbirds in the leaves
Or soothe a woeful lover's cares.

I think about my Spring that dies
The while I dream of things to come;
My past is only memories
Which will, alas, become my tomb.

A Work Woman's Song

To Denys Lanctôt

Like a bomb fortunes split;
The falling day is hit;
Hope and trust are mixed with it.

Prick-needle! pricked enough, stung!
    Like a bomb fortunes split.

Here all things whine, weep, quit.
Nothing we do could fit
The past when we lived in it.

Prick-needle! pricked enough, stung!
Here all things whine, weep, quit.

I tire of the days I spend,
I want to sleep, good friend,
Let me rest and make an end.

No, prick-needle! pricked enough stung!
I tire of the days I spend.

Gaunt from my hard day's toil
I curse my fate's turmoil,
A pale leaf in the wind's rout;

Blood down my finger flows,
The hour gasps, mourns, and goes,
My bread sticks in my throat.

No matter, prick-needle, pricked, stung!
The hour gasps, mourns, and goes.

Why does God give me this fate?
Like a pig's is my poor state.
Sorrow is a heavy weight.

No matter, prick-needle, pricked, stung!
Why does God give me this fate?

All neglected do I pass.
My bread I gain or lose
In one whirl of giddiness.

No matter, prick-needle! pricked, stung!
All neglected do I pass.

Nocturne

To Denys Lanctôt

It is the solemn time that silence keeps,
The Angelus tolls our prayers to God's face;
In deep long rest the heart, believing, sleeps,
Drowned in the flat perfumes of the Holy Place.

It is sorrow-time when the sinner weeps;
It is a time when we vow our purer grace,
When our eye, wet with recognition's tears, keeps
The fiery zeal it had in the first place.

O night so easeful for my heart's agony,
Night of mercy to a sinner suffering
Who asks for manna from God's charity,

Possess with your shade a soul in torment cast,
The past's communion sudden in your breast,
That it may have joy and peace when Matins ring.

Hearts Blasé

In the last dark night of all, their eyes fade;
They wished for life and hunted out a dream;
But for their blaspheming hearts, whence all hope
    fled,
They never found the right true-flowing stream.

Vainly they sought to kill the soul in vice;
Awed, it still remains, Remorse's agony.
A pale angel stands, by their left hands' space,
To tear their gasping hearts until they die.

A Rubinstein Melody

Like the echo of a sacred concert played,
One hears it suddenly and does not understand;
As when the soul in hashish smoke is drowned
To make a grief that cannot be repaid.

From these soft bars, their suffering hearts
    betrayed
By much-loved music like a tender hope
That always leaves, still meandering to grope
In the chill void where their sleeping nerves are
    laid,

They have understood nothing except one
Great dream, where, without intermission,
Some warm feelings the melody brings back

Deep in their hearts. In the melancholy
Chords they remember that soft passion
Which good luck builds and which their love songs
    lack.

Charles Baudelaire

Master of great verse, poet without equal,
You charm us with a grace both new and grand;
Parnassian wizard, wizard from the sun's gold
    land,
Our language sighs beneath your harp-notes
    lyrical.

The Classics were dead; behold they wake as well;
Great Reviver, under your pure wings' spread
A whole age groups. In your cup of verses red
We drink sweet poison that holds us in its spell.

Verlaine and Mallarmé have taken your trail.
Master, though dead, you will be living still;
You will live on, in a full and replete day.

From the Past your century opens a way
Where, pearls of your waning, flowers will be
    reborn.
Behold the Night ends with the wakening Morn.

Beatrice

At first I saw an oaken cradle where
A sleepless baby roared in raucous key
Until a black-eyed grandchild entered there,

A pale, dark girl from pleasure's bondage free.

Dreamy is her brow; haughty is her air
In a white dress that fits her beautifully;
Her charm is goodness; all her mild soul's care
Is sinless truth that will not cease to be.

Dear child, let your life flow on in this way;
Help, pray, believe; console those in misery.
May this short song be your sweet melody!

I lift my gaze toward the sky-blue dome
Where the stars swim in night's ethereal home,
Finding you more pure than their purest ray.

1897
Old Piano

In this old instrument the soul no more
Vibrates. Its closed lid gives it a look of gloom;
In shade it sleeps, banned from the drawing-room,
This misanthrope, in isolation sour.

I remember all those nocturnes then
That my mother played, and mourn in dreams
Those long-past nights — gone in their shadowy
        gleams —
Of sadly rendered Liszt and faint Beethoven.

My life's image, O old black piano;
Like you my soul from joy is forced to go.
You lack an artist, and I lack an ideal.

There you sleep, the world's one joy I still can feel.
O deep distress, who will return to tease
A triumphant concert from your dying keys?

Monks in Procession

Heads bowed, they pace the length of ancient
      aisles,
Fingering great rosaries of polished wood
As the evening sun from its beams' red blood
Crimsons in splendour the monastic tiles.

Already now the hour has in its toils
Of ecstatic flame their great hearts, where secrets
Of disgust with human-kind, where regrets
And the tame thrill of starved flesh have domiciles.

They walk through the night; nothing moves them
      at all,
Not even the horrible shadows of fire
That follow them on the walls to the church door,

Not even that mean spirit's infernal call
Who tempts, supreme in his rebellious arts,
All these, Jesus Christ's own ghostly counterparts.

Evening Rhythms

See how the tulip, dahlia, and the rose
Among basins, bronzes, statuaries
In great parks where Love sports beneath the trees
Sing in blue eves, pink and monotonous.

In blue eves, the flower-beds sing their joyous
      chords
When the moonlight's dance is a shifting show,
And when briskly the gales their sad notes blow,
Troubling the pure dreams of solitary birds.

See how the tulip, dahlia, and the rose,
And crystal lilies enamoured of twilight,

86

Turn pale and sad to the sun in its flight
That bears away from beasts and things their woes.

See now how the dahlia, like love's red wound,
Awaits the clear morn's kisses cool and rose;
See how the lily, tulip, and the rose
Mourn the memories with which my soul is
    drowned.

The Traveller

To my father

Tired of viewing peoples, continents, and towns
And seeing palaces, monuments and skies,
The traveller returns to the familiar downs
And laughing vales he loved in younger days.

Under ancient oaks, a few good rustic clowns
On old benches, when the night-time easy lies,
Gravely smoke their pipes near their relations
And hear tall stories from the white-haired wise.

Spring blooms again. The inconstant nightingale
In his rustic palace resumes his trill.
But benches are empty; for man is abroad.

He can be seen no more on his native sod.
He disappeared in the night, a phantom cast
On the mortal breath of a wintry blast.

Sculptor in Marble

A massive sculpture deep in the studio
Stands, a statue with a marble pedestal,

As the rosy dawn on its stature tall
Casts crimson beams through the stained-glass
    window.

How many nights into a likeness go
Made real by a tormented spirit's toil!
A confused visage in its great turmoil
Is turned to prize in this allegoric show.

A genial breath takes hold upon your heart
And thrills the length of that colossal body,
Grim Reaper firm at his task eternally;

A Bacchus lies prone; and each visitor
Sees, arms on the cross, that sublime sculptor,
Death at Death's feet, his last great work of art.

1898
Golden Sonnet

In this triumphant night the coldness dies
And the divine currents of Spring reappear;
Winter is gone, for April's gardener
In his flower-harem has chosen his prize.

Open your shutters and let the drunk airs rise
And mingle with a heaven rosy pure
To reach this room where our love reigns secure
With soft sounds that on your lute you improvise.

Allegro, Yvette, allegro: I prefer
To get drunk on the glad bird-song I hear
Than hark to your ivory key-board's moan.

Let's dream in a green park now the ice is gone;
You can tell me whether this glorious April
Is worth all the work of Mozart and Handel.

On A Portrait of Dante

It is he, that face whose smile is all its own,
That brow blackened by the hot wind of hell,
That eye where dreams sublime are swimming still,
Incomparable Dante, a man unknown.

Your mighty soul that all our minds have known,
Its style removed from rascals' jealousies,
On eternal mountains where you touched the skies
Should find, O guileless bard, for peace a throne.

Guardian of graveyards, sublime Alighieri,
On the wall of time the glorious blazonry
Of your proud works flames up indelible,

And you will live, O Dante, like God in them;
For heaven has learned as well as hell
To read the lines of your divine poem.

Ecclesiastical Siesta

A Summer Sketch

In his new soutane he looks fine indeed,
This plump little priest, fresh shaven as well,
For whom good food weaves an innocent spell

          . . .
He dreams of it under the plane-tree's shade.

Noon rings a bell. The sun struts overhead,
And monsieur the vicar, O scandalous view!
Lies drunk on the lawn, and abstracted, too,
Musing on doings in some harlot's bed.

Then comes the food . . . under white cloth,
          Blanche, Louise,
Michel, and verger nudge one another's knees,
As they all go off in gales of laughter,

89

While the priest, in no way sorry after,
Stretches, then murmurs, with heavenly grin,
How Bacchus, too, was a good Christian man.

Easter Communion

Sweets, mystical sweets! O the sweets that mourn!
Has the blue sky dropped into our hearts' sad
    bourne?

The whole heaven, this Sabbath, at the Easter
    mass,
Makes the thick dark mist of our sadness pass;

Full of angels, incense-bearers triumphal,
Bearing their urns of peace and joy to all;

When the concert of Saint Cecilia sounds
That the organ now in pious fulness rounds,

Could it be that a new Eden moved us there
While the *Sanctus* made us kneel in prayer?

And while, under their dewy gleams, our eyes
Became soul-mirrors in seraphic guise,

In the glad morning, among stained-glass windows,
Whose glory joins the gold of the saints' haloes?

Whence do you come, in mystic religion caught,
Whose sweet ecstasy makes earth an alien spot?

Is it not that delightful hour, O Faith,
When, as scriptures say, Christ, revived from
    death,

For Himself revives our souls, all damp and drear,
By the small sunbeams of the Hosts of Easter.

Small Stained-Glass Window

Jesus, blonde-bearded and with eyes of soft
     sapphire,
Amid the sacred flight of singing cherubim,
Who bend toward Him to love Him and to hear
     Him,
Smiles in an old stained-glass window of the
     defunct choir.
The birds of Zion with wings translucent and calm
Are there in sunbeams whose dust-motes flash like
     wildfire,
And it is as sweet as a poet's song on the lyre
To see them so, among fine arabesques of palm,
In this small stained-glass window when the
     sunbeams expire
Amid the sacred flight of singing cherubim,
Smiling in the choir, a glory more than words can
     limn,
Christ, with his golden beard and eyes of soft
     sapphire.

The Benedictine

Three months after the convent first saw her
While divine desire grew in her being still,
A handsome bird, stopping at her window-sill,
Built its nest on it, then made its dwelling there.

There it lived and ate for many a year,
But, since she oft felt reborn this world's dull chill,
To its neck she tied some words of wayward
     will . .
She then grew calm, but the bird returned no more.

Snowing down on the Benedictine, old age
Made her, one silver night, her soul disengage,
Eyes raised in growing joy up to the skies:

When to a strange chorus she reached heaven's
     throne,
She saw, demanding her seat in paradise,
The bird that to God's hands her letter had flown!

Fra Angelico

To Madame W.Y., Hately

Angelico laboured from his matins on
To bring to light the vision that he bore;
Painting the Virgin with such portraiture
As no Florentine oils had ever known.

That is why the awe-struck prior, vespers done,
Oft saw him in the nave in dream-stupor;
Angelico laboured from his matins on
To bring to light the vision that he bore.

Then in his cell one night while bells rang on,
They found the artist fainting on the floor;
Under his robe a masterpiece he bore
Which an angel from Sistine skies had sent down

To aid his brother's toil from matins on.

1902
Fragments

I

VISION

And now I dream of shadows stained with blood,
Proud prancing steeds; the sounds I hear

92

Are like children's coughs, cries of tramps' despair,
    Death-rattles of the slowly dead.

Where are they from, those horns that blare and
        blow,
    Snare-drum or fife in noisy wars?
It could be said that through the town, hussars
    Gallop with sea-green helms aglow.

II

THE DEATH OF PRAYER

There come to him, like reproaches that from
        heaven fall,
Angelically sad and sweet, the pleas
That call him back to prayer . . . the chapel bell!
But Arouet is there and grips his knees.

III

THE MADMAN

Addlepate! Addlepate!
You no longer travel late.

They have murdered poor folly,
They crushed him under a trolley,
And then his dog after folly.

They dug them a big hole in the sod.
    It's the God of wrath, it's that God.
Kneel down at that hole in the sod.

IV

THE EVENING

The evening seeds Love, and solemn litanies
    With that dream fall on their knees.

V

I PLACE

Softly I place the deformed fingers of my moods
Laden with the black rings of my worldly loathing
Upon the dark keyboard of life and all its goods.

VI

I FEEL FLYING

I feel the birds of genius flying in me,
But I set my trap so clumsily that they flew,
All white, brown, and grey, into the cerebral blue
And left my broken heart gasping its agony.

VII

LET'S TAMP THE ROAD-TURN

Let's tamp the road-turn
Almost reborn
To our ghost passing forlorn.

Come now, let us chat
About this and that
Of the villa's old format.

Among voices stilled
Of statues eld
All helter-skelter spilled.

A park dead and gone
Where scents hang on
Of nights both white and brown. . . .

After 1904
To A Hated Woman

How I hate you and how I flee from you:
All the same your beauty you most nobly bear;
The angels must have made your long flowing hair
And those glances with night's dark charm in their
     hue.

Never since the time when first you wounded me
Could I ease that inner burn: flighty creature,
You hurt me more than any man can endure
As in me snarled my volcanic misery.

I, madam, with no love except for Art,
And you soulless, indifferent, cold,
Let us not meet; let us, apart, grow old.

Before your charms I ought not to bend my brow;
Only explain the sadness in my heart
That makes me want to cry this evening now.

The Sad Wind of Autumn

With a cry like that from an infant's throat,
Dismal, triumphant, the wind through the woods
Races and tears through the bark that it shreds,
Mixing its distant cries with the horn's low note.

See how it eases; its furies sleep and drowse
Like playtime in the dark night's tenderness;
Its violin lulled our dreams of happiness
That give their fragrance to the flowering boughs.

Like it, rising inevitably to bray
And rage, yet often holding your tongue as well,
Woman, your love is the wind's parallel.

Before it strikes our souls, it strokes us lightly;
After it gets in to crush us, comes a day
When it will weep over our hearts' strewn debris!

To George Rodenbach

White, all white, O Swan, your pale wings unbare,
You soar to your native Eden repossessed,
Far from your Flemish land with its grey-fog breast
And those dead towns whose death-throes are your
    despair.

Bruges, where do those black-shawled widows go
    down there?
By your bells be told your grief to heaven high!
Along your broad canals with melancholy
Let knells fly out, bronze crows in windless air.

Meanwhile towards the north, a blue sky shines
To become, as mere words say, a golden light,
O Flanders, dazzling all your dismal sight.

You nuns who pray in the offices of night,
From the monstrance lift your eyes and
    contemplate
That mystic Choice of all eternal dawns!

The Wreath

Sadness tonight engulfs me in its lair
As through the dark calm of streets I wander,
Eluding the growing crowds and their clamour,
To see a great wreath hanging on a door.

While lying on the dead-man's threshold there
I see the thoughts of mischief sordid, raw,

And of struggles gone, a panorama
That the world in its way chooses to ignore.

Good or bad passer-by, whoever you are,
My brother, if you see this emblem of grief,
Uncover your head as soon as you can,

And think, greeting death that will take us all in,
How each hour is but a thread for a wreath
That may be laid tomorrow at your door.

A Poet

Let him live then and harm not anything!
Let him depart, a dreamer passing by,
An angel soul, open to infinity,
Bearing his own dawn of celestial Spring.

There is a poetry both sad and pure
Rising from him in a gold storm that sweeps.
The star can understand, that star which sleeps
In twinkling lace of heaven's white allure.

He wants to know nothing; loves without reply.
Don't look at him! There's nothing there to see!
Call him the fool of his own destiny!
Laugh at him . . . So what? One day he has to
    die . . .

In heaven where the good Lord lives alway,
With bitter blame, you will be taught to know
What truth there was inside that plain proud brow,
What sadness in those weeping eyes of grey!

Chopin's Tomb

Sleep, far from the Floriani's kisses untrue,
O pale consumptive, amid French laurels now!

A bit of natal earth is one with your woe,
The Palatine soil that was provided you.

When you came, Chopin, with dreams no one
      knew,
A great hope bloomed on your thin countenance
To do for your art what in the Renaissance
Of Florence many painters accomplished, too.

Like a funeral lily envased in pride
You bend, young man, knowing no more to
      swallow . . .
From the tomb the harpsichord beats out your
      stride.

Sleep, Chopin, may the green bending willow
Cast its shade on your sleep sad and beautiful,
A child of Poland in the gold arms of Gaul!

Cradle-Song

Some one mourns in the bleak calm
      Of nights in April;
Some one mourns the long sleep-time
      Of his own exile.
Some one mourns his misery
      And that's the heart in me . . .

German Parlours

Yet in my mind these huge still rooms I hold,
Full of worn-out velvet, thoughtful ancestors,
And guests under the sway of bright chandeliers
Who moved through minuets and in waltzes rolled.

I think of portraits done in days of old
Hung over hearths that seemed, in death's slow
      speech,
To ask us: Why do you, living, laugh so much?
And Goethe's poems in cultured nights of gold.

I recall Dutch paintings, artists who dream
Sadly as they sit and blow their smoke rings higher
While their eyes are turned toward a friendly fire.

I mourn, but know not how to end the theme.
See now how I hear, singing on the stair,
An old Magyar tenor with long powdered hair.

Posthumous Poems

The Tomb of Charles Baudelaire

I dream of a terrible and lunar tomb
Without movement or feeling, placed in the sky,
And a fixed flame — to which the world would
      pray —
To make sublime in glory myth and gnome.

It is built out of words that easy come
Somewhere in Troy or in the Milky Way,
An elf in the sky, a ragman would say,
Settling the scraps in our planetary home.

O unsought singer of sun-lit lands, begin;
Let your poems glorious beyond equal
Be a gravestone fit for Charles Baudelaire.

I bow as I pass before it there,
And dream an aurora borealis violin
To worship in verse forever musical.

I Know Down There . . .

I know down there a pink maiden
      With big soft eyes, a Danube flower
O so fine that in the region
      A rose-bud is jealous of her.

She flowered one evening pure,
    In a magic harmony
With a high sky of pale azure:
    She is the pride of Romany.

Little Hamlet

See how a hamlet grows green on its hills
Girded with holly, and proud of the height of
    its ills.

The shepherds with wonder keep watch on the
    plains
And my horse sweating up high draws in on its
    reins.

To follow October and its pastoral calms
I bring you, O Pan, my evening psalms.

The steers are soon stalled. They low in the stable,
And the steam of good soup has delighted my
    table.

How happy you are, good countrymen, who dwell
Far from the stink of the suburb and shouts of the
    jail.

I bless you. May joy live at your door swung wide
To the open, O those nights when the first leaves
    died!

Red Dawn

Dawn bursts in a bloody spray
    Upon the mist-covered hills

As a low mooing trembles our way
    From an ox with steaming nostrils.

It is the time for butchering.
　　Holding him by the halter still

The lads tie his neck in a cloth ring
　　To mark him for the next kill.

The axe falls with such a fearful plaint
　　That they pause against their mood

Procumbit bos. Like an elephant
　　Toppling in a solitude.

The blood bursts forth. Down the horns it flows.
　　The sun makes a hideous red stain

And Phoebus sings to the sad bellows
　　Of an ox broken in twain.

Modern Pan

Seven goats make his patrimony;
When the dawn-air in his lungs thrills
We see him passing through the hills,
Flute to lips, a good deity.

Straighter than a yew, his rib-cage
Is shafted in eternal air;
His eye slays demons everywhere
And bears, like hares, flee from his rage.

The pride of all goatherds is he,
And, like an old roebuck, his brow
Has dared the thunder without fear.

As his life, so will his death be,
Upright and chaste, without a sou.
I drink to Fritz in his hundredth year!

Virgilian

October spreads its evening calm and pale
    Like a dead mother's shade.

The goatherds seem to mock the stirring gale
    By the way their pipes are played.

But one is still. From his lips the instrument
    Suddenly falls by my feet.

He knows I love his goats from the times we went
    Chatting on evenings late.

I respect him as an old old man, but more
    On my part as rustic gold.

This centenarian has filled with his lore
    My own sad heart's deep hold.

Let us awaken often when the brown night glows
    To intervals soft yet strong

Of a piping that bleats to the holly boughs
    By moonlight its ancient song.

Rural Chateau

I had this dream. She is twenty. I am no less;
    We'll live in any lovely place
        That her affections bless.

It will be all meadow, save the base of the vale;
    We shall have three-fold carnival:
        House, cock, and horse in stall.

She is blue-eyed; therefore all things will be blue;
    Gable, frame, threshold, door, all blue:
        Maybe inside a bit, too.

She had blonde hair; we shall garner wheat-ears,
   Sunlight, springtime, fine days, grass, flowers
      And love that has no cares.

No doubt, she will have me, seeing my misery —
   Were it only but to flout me —
      An angelic deputy!

Abruptly I wake. Down there in the young dawn
   A rural Frenchman starts to mourn
      His Spanish henhouse gone!

How Sadly Sounds . . .

In October how sadly sounds with crimson swell
   The Vesper bell!

Its weary obsequies enamoured of the doom
   Of too great gloom!

In a chamber white and rose, a maiden white and rose
   Takes her repose.

And the hamlet is still. But returning herdsmen
   Remember then

In the foothills amid their songs of earlier days
   All her ways

In other times with them. An angel bucolic,
   And a relic

Of childhood forever sweet! One man is dumb.
   Fritz is his name.

For that goatherd, king of the flocks that stray
   Near by the bay,

Loved her. Now he mourns for her! He was her
    shield-rock,
        A rigid block

Whose simple strength outwore every file of time.
    There the sublime

Old man mourned her death like a snowflake come
    and gone.
        A procession

Took shape. Two heavy arms bear her to a chapel,
    And a shovel

Ploughs underground an exile from the life-tide
    Whose every stride

My sad steps have followed. She lies there, all
    alone,
        In earth deep down.

I hear her in my dreams. She mourns in the bells'
    tone
        From evening on.

I have kept a fraternal memory of her,
    One struggle dear

With another of yesteryear. Grief is not with me
    Green. It is dry

From that flame which in the coal of its furnace-
    fire
        Embraces her.

My grief is such I could drink up worlds and swill
    Their waves at will.

My grief where in silence like a potted lily
    I inward die . . .

In October how sadly sounds with crimson swell
      The Vesper bell! . . .

Many Nights

Many nights we wander in the vale
Where the grey hours go, mourning-wise.
Tears pearl her bright sorb-apple eyes
As she hears the *Cydalises*
Of that god whose name was Nerval.

Ah! Should she in a long flight of gold
Rejoin them in domains more vast
Than any court that Rome can boast,
Where through eternal weeks in slumber fast
Lies the cup of delights untold;

Or should she open her vernal parts
To furies of deadly cyclones
Which crumble, like the columned stones
Among the so-chaste Babylons
That inhabit all young girls' hearts?

Yes, dear, how fine is your heart's bloom!
Let swift innocent days fall there;
Flee from the town, its plagues ignore,
You will be near to heaven the more
You are far away from its tomb.

I'd Like to Dodge Myself

I'd like to dodge myself in some
Brusque throng of sudden gaiety.
Yes, I would deceive even me
In cyclones of delirium.

What grim vampires, you, who fearsome
Go, sucking the heart out of me!
I want to be mad, if only
To flout Distresses should they come!

Softly, like a huge cadaver,
My heart is moored in the harbour
With all the heteromorphic louts.

Let me bless those bestial snouts
Whose wild laughter void of sense
Jeers at the maid, Intelligence!

Sad Prelude

I opened my heart to you, a cathedral
Where of old your hands swung thuribles
In those days when I wore hope's chasubles,
Playing in my white room near my mother's call.

How sadly now on me those memories fall
And what dark toys my ennuis become!
I leave alone. Through nights and days I roam.
They say, Go. I go without a word at all.

I am alone. I find life both sad and sweet.
For me the world is like some huge winding-sheet
Whence suddenly for strange reasons I shall rise,

All deathly ill and mad beyond control,
To murmur soft angelic melodies,
After that to leave, then die inside my hole.

To Sister with Love

Say, Death, what do you do with those trophies
        grand

Of maids that burn our fires on altars high?
Speak: When shall we defy mortality
In bright abodes where heaven's Urals stand?

I lived an ideal. She was in fairyland! . . .
I am not sure, but her eyes were so bright
There I saw tall castles growing in the night,
Massive-proud, with parks and grottos close at
        hand.

It is night. Let's go through the wood, my dear.
We two shall follow on the hard rough road
That leads to the chapel of yesteryear.

My voice calls you, sister, but your gold tones
Elude me. Yesterday Gertrude died. My moans
Are like empty bells in the solitude.

Brother Alfus

I

Old brother Alfus, the monk of this story,
Lived in a chaste, humble, mild, and learned way
At Olmutz in an old monastery.

Through many wastes his renown had its day
For Science had given him a mighty dower
And his spirit was full of learning's sway.

From all sides, men who loved him came to his
        bower;
His head turned white from the frost in his brain
But his thought stuck at a point without power.

He heard the spring, the bird, then the wind run on;
But to solve the mystery brought on despair:
Pensive still, he returned to the convent lawn.

Like a tree he bent over the parterre.
Little by little a storm brewed in his soul,
For like a rough volcano Doubt gnawed there.

Pride's sword his humble faith did disembowel;
The old monk went, bearing on his shoulders all
The griefs that hell could doubtless there uproll.

Sometimes he mused, walking under willows tall,
Missal in hand, finger on his temple hot,
That maybe God and man were nothing at all.

What use to us, now that our sins are caught,
Under hair-shirts chaste to curb our longings crude
And live like dead men for a heaven that is not?

His heart conferred with baneful voices lewd.
The sky, the bird, the tree, the earth were glad,
But the monk was sad, deep in this vast wood.

II

THE VOICE IN THE VISION

Now one day when he went, doubting the skies
And the infinity of all they bless,
A far-off heaven half-opened to his eyes

And his brow, all furrowed by learning's stress,
Dazed and quivering, perceived suddenly
An angelic heath in rosy loneliness.

A great angel on a night of wizardry,
God's son, came down from heaven's Sistine hill.
In a dream he showed his magic land to me.

A place with silver moons. A landscape still
Like that the monk Angelico dreamed for hours
In the nave as Latin prayers uprose at will.

When a dry wind prowls with its ivory flowers
This whole Eden trembles with a sacred song
That to a hundred skies re-echoes in showers.

And stillness is sweet in the soft winds' song
And a great calm falls like a blue embrace
On magic that lies where sleeping fountains throng.

And the air is flecked with a fiery grace
And heaven's breath descends as spirals curl
Around brother Alfus who sleeps for a space.

Under flowery moss the evening springs purl.
Quivering in their chill jar to the moan
Of starry harps, the gold mackerel swirl.

Then suddenly swells a musical tone.
The voice of a bluebird softens the sleep
Of that monk from the monkish pathway gone.

It rings out loud through silence far and deep
Like a pure and slowly modulated wound
To the abashed doubt that too-proud humans
        keep.

See how, approaching with a controlled sound,
In his ear she pours her hymn, there to knell
Its sudden song one hundred years around.

Then a great harmony like the sea's swell
Falls from out the bird's celestial bill.
Softly she reveals the heart of the marvel:

"Alfus, my son, under this divine hill
I let you sleep where my choric song beguiles,
More sweet than songs heard in your mother's
        cradle.

"Asleep in the boughy peace of woodland aisles
You lie broken, full of a passing pride
In the peace of these terrestrial exiles.

"Return to earth. One moment there reside
If only to put in disarray your Doubt.
Return to earth. Leave this land where none has
    died."

Then Alfus, waking, saw his dream fade out,
Ending in song. He was seized with alarm
And Sun and Dawn were there to powder his route.

III

RETURN TO THE MONASTERY

"How everything has changed. I find a flaw
On this road where yesterday I chanced to go.
All has died, as one would deem, by some strange
    law.

"Am I mad, O God, what means this dawning's
    glow?
I left my old convent earlier today.
What change takes place whose rules I do not
    know,

"The wood's no longer there. But these women,
    they
Did not come to draw water alone before.
Tell me, peasant, am I on the Olmutz way?"

The speaker has a form and face austere.
He wears the good friars of Olmutz' cloak
As though the new convent were now not there.

The puzzled gardener, elbow on his rake,
Halts. They watch each other in amazement.
The angelus bells through the hillside quake.

Over the threshold of worn stones Alfus went.
He knew at last that a miracle had come
And he in sleep a hundred years had spent.

"Alfus . . ." an old man remembered the name.
"Alfus . . . before I as a novice stood
I heard of that lost brother, all the same.

"He was a mild monk who sought for pleasure
        good
In peace, prayer, and a holy flame's reward.
One dawn, for his pains, he got lost in the wood.

"Though they searched everywhere, turned many
        a sward,
Never of him could they find a single thing.
Deeming him dead, they left him to the Lord."

Then, raising his eyes as at an offering,
The saint died, cleansed of doubt. The chosen one,
The old monk Alfus round whom legends ring.

If heaven so wills, for us, too, let it be done.

The Suicide of Angel Valdor

To Wilfred Larose

I

In April old Angel Valdor was wed
In the nave to one with black eyes and blonde
        head.

The sunlight smote, with crimson-shafted furor,
The stained-glass, that praying angels' mirror.

Seeing them leave triumphant, everywhere
People said that they would live without a care,

That their love would be like a Sunday temple
Where love presided in a white chasuble.

In the nave in April the bellringer wed
His young fiancée with black eyes and blonde head.

II

For a long time his heart was free and glad;
In his eyes hymeneal roses blossomed red.

He lived on woman's kisses that too much lied
Until the day his heart a vile doubt supplied.

He asked of heaven a boy with eyes of brown
Who would replace him when he was dead and
    gone,

And who would make ring from their tall towers
The bells that now he tolled with puny powers.

When Maytime came his heart was free and glad;
In his eyes hymeneal roses blossomed red.

III

But in June the bellringer began to grieve
And often went to his garden at eve,

Pensive, walking full of doubt and care's load . . .
One might say his love's train had left the road.

To a star he confided some of his woe
Blacker than the black flight of a vesper crow.

113

Care and grief prostrated all his courage,
He felt himself swell with a slow rage.

That was why, in June, without a by-your-leave
He went alone in his garden at eve.

IV

By October the bellringer's love was done,
And he went, his eyes mad like a moon-struck man.

His faithless wife, oh the crazy swallow!
Had now fled his hearth, faithless to her vow,

Cheating the love of old Angel Valdor
Who walked alive with heart dead at its core,

From his empty silent home, moving down
To the distant slums of a garish town.

In mournful October his love was done:
And his the gruesome walk of a moon-struck man.

V

After having rung the Angelus, Valdor
Took at eve the stair to the black bell tower.

The scrape of his shoes echoed death-rattles hoarse
Amid the tower under the pale stars' course.

The basilica's sides trembled where they stood
And its stained-glass windows shone red like
        blood,

And the doors, grating on a hinge of iron,
Carried the knell of a funeral omen.

There rang three chords abruptly when Valdor
That evening climbed in the grim black tower.

114

Then November fell with its woes forlorn . . .
This is a black tale for the loves I mourn . . .

The bishop at dawn, reaching the cursed towers,
Stayed there a long time, with suspended powers,

Before the hanging corpse on the belfry rope,
The cold bellringer's corpse, twisted beyond hope.

Weird were the prayers that the priest besought
For that poor soul in devil-fingers caught,

For the ringer, and for his cruel wife as well,
Whose knell Valdor tolled with the bells of hell.

Cats

To dead gas-burners, in the house, at night,
They often prolong eternal cries;
Nor can we sink into their blue-green eyes
And plumb their mystic lethal sense of right.

Sometimes their backs, too, fluff and shiver
As their live fur bristles its streams of sparks
Toward the dire midnights of solemn clocks
They hear, striking with an eerie shiver.

The Deadly Cat

One night as I scanned many a volume,
Seeking a dark token of deep gloom
A phantom cat drew near me in the room
      And suddenly pounced on me;
In such a manner then he pounced on me
That since that time I've known continually

Such a spasm of immortal agony
        As is hell's marriage fee.

I was sad, of course, and drunken, too,
And looked into the book that I might know
What things there were to rescue here below
        From all our bitter care.
He told me then with utmost emphasis
That all I sought was but an empty phrase,
That I was drunk in an ecstatic haze
        And dreaming on my chair.

I stood up in the litter of my room.
I was drunk and also filled with gloom.
From shadows deep I saw him, prancing, loom,
        I waved my heart quite bravely;
And thus I mourned: "O demon grim and stern,
Go now away and in the dark return."
But he, in a manner that all cats learn,
        Arched his back to mock me.

My command put him in such a laughing fit
That I was seized with rage because of it,
And I with wrathful heart inflamed fell flat
        On the carpet rolling.
Alertly then the cat snapped up his prey.
He ate my heart and then he went away
With open jaws, proud of my life's decay,
        With pleasure mewling.

From that old-time flight this fantastic guest
Remained I would have killed if unpossessed
By fear that took the heart from out my breast
        And truly laid me low;
He would have joined my list of dead things then
Had I had hands with strength enough to win.

Ah! but I knock against the gate in vain
　　Of my gigantic woe.

All the same, however, sometimes I pause
To consider the poor heart his tooth gnaws
And will gnaw while time is caught in the jaws
　　Of all the lies we are
And womenkind are proven all untrue.
Since I fit so well into your black shoe,
O Life, open your pit for me, too,
　　To dance forever there.

I am overwhelmed by this cat-terror,
And I know it will soon give me grey hair;
Only to think of his kinky black fur
　　Makes my chill body twist.
And now, filled with emotion's sharp turmoil,
With my hair standing stiff from fright as well,
I traverse my room, stale with the sick smell
　　Of horror from the past.

Mortals, you smooth-skinned souls of simpletons,
You, too, will have these fine celebrations,
You will lose your hearts and let your heads be
　　pawns
　　When the devil appears,
Clawing you all the way he once clawed me,
As he did on that night of misery
When I set to rhyme the strange history
　　Of the cat of my Despairs.

The Spectre

Through all my winter eves he sat
In my chair of green velvet
　　Near to the hearth;

Smoking my pipe of thin-glazed earth,
He sat, a spectre tall in height,
Under the dying coals of light
Behind my screen's funereal blight.

He has haunted, like a pale ghost,
My dark hovel, and his accursed
        soliloquys
Have filled it with strange maladies.
Speak freely, spectre, your name indite
That is bound to wrench my heart outright
Behind my screen's funereal blight.

When I asked his name, the skeleton
Bellowed like a mighty cannon
        And bit the blue
Veins of his lips almost in two.
With his face inclined, he stood upright
And his wild howl had force to smite
Behind my screen's funereal blight.

"In your awful nights you call me
The spectre of your ennui,
        O brother mine.
To my sad breast your breast consign
That I may press it with my might
And triumph at the hour, right
Behind my screen's funereal blight."

By fiery eye and madness stung,
He gnashed his teeth and then unslung
        A sash from his throat.
With bony fingers, like harpstrings mute,
Thin saffron-yellow in the light,
He hooked my heart in his grim bite
Behind the screen's funereal blight.

The Terrace with its Spectres

When the dismal terrace again I see
Where turrets bristle from a haunt chateau,
The nameless fear of ghosts from long ago
Crosses my whole being and flattens me.

My eye touches, as Dante was wont to see,
At eve some weird and wandering nearby glow
When the dismal terrace again I see
Where turrets bristle from a haunt chateau.

A hellish race returns posthumously
There to sing its loves to the trumpet's roar,
Beldames and knights in funeral attire
Eclipsed without trace as day dawns free

When the dismal terrace again I see

Black Virgin

Her eyes are like strange torches in a room.
Down her frail shoulders hair of phoney gold,
Like willow leaves a-tremble in the cold,
Falls to clothe her as cypress clothes a tomb.

And as she walks, her clothes turn rags, illume
Swart ugliness; whether immured in jail
Or beaten soundly with great rods of steel,
Mortals, beware: she's meat the crows consume.

With such sincere goodwill her smile was blithe,
I could have thought her kind and free from care
And that we could embrace each other there.

But when I spoke, dark longing in my eyes,
She said, "Your feet have dirtied all my ways."
Surely you must know her; her name is Life.

Hypochondriac Nights

Sometimes I strike my livid brow,
Impelled by nameless tragic fears
When the harpsichord is twanging low

And the pale, swaying chandeliers
Flash their beams on all my woe
As sad sounds fall dark upon my ears.

With scarce-hid tears my two eyes flow;
Senseless through rooms I take my flight
Only to find what sad hello:

Great frosts now freeze my limbs outright;
I seek for death to set me free
Through sad December's baleful night!

Accursed angels, please help me!